CONFESSIONS OF A FAST WOMAN

Other books by Lesley Hazleton:

ENGLAND, BLOODY ENGLAND:
An Expatriate's Return

JERUSALEM, JERUSALEM

THE RIGHT TO FEEL BAD:
Coming to Terms with Normal Depression

WHERE MOUNTAINS ROAR:
A Personal Report from the Sinai and Negev Desert

ISRAELI WOMEN:
The Reality Behind the Myths

CONFESSIONS OF A

Fast Woman

LESLEY HAZLETON

Addison-Wesley Publishing Company

READING, MASSACHUSETTS MENLO PARK, CALIFORNIA NEW YORK
DON MILLS, ONTARIO WOKINGHAM, ENGLAND AMSTERDAM BONN
SYDNEY SINGAPORE TOKYO MADRID SAN JUAN
PARIS SEOUL MILAN MEXICO CITY TAIPEI

Many of the designations used by manufacturers and sellers to distinguish their products are claimed as trademarks. Where those designations appear in this book and Addison–Wesley was aware of a trademark claim, the designations have been printed in initial capital letters (e.g., Porsche).

Library of Congress Cataloging-in-Publication Data

Hazleton, Lesley.
    Confessions of a fast woman / Lesley Hazleton.
        p.   cm.
    ISBN 0-201-63204-7
    1. Automobile drivers--Psychology. 2. Automobiles--Speed-
-Psychological aspects. 3. Hazleton, Lesley--Psychology.
I. Title.
TL152.3.H39 1992
629.28'3'019--dc20
                                                                    92-9785
                                                                    CIP

Jacket design by Designed to Print & Assoc.
Jacket illustration by Hide Muramatsu
Text design by C. Linda Dingler
Set in 10.5-point Goudy by CopyRight, Inc.

1 2 3 4 5 6 7 8 9-MW-95949392
First printing, July 1992

To my parents,
Sybil and Jessel,
with love and thanks

CONTENTS

I

DISCOVERING

THE

DAEMON

I

IT BEGAN IN THE SPRING OF 1988. That was when I first drove at twice the speed limit. I was in a Porsche 911, and I'd never been in one before. It was a revelation. In fact, it was a seduction.

I'd find out later that the 911 was nearly as close as you could come in a production car to the feeling of driving a race car. But I knew nothing about cars at the time, let alone race cars. All I knew was that I liked to drive. And that as I worked my way through the gears, some force seemed to rise out of the engine—out of the road itself—and enter me, body and soul.

I'd always thought of cars as mere machinery, but this one made me think of animals—fast, lithe ones like racehorses and panthers. It felt alive beneath my hands, some metal creature bred for wind and speed. At low speed in town, it didn't take much to imagine that it was prancing and snorting, aching for the open road, so I took it north into Vermont, and once the highway cleared, I shifted down, ran quickly up to the engine howl of 7,000 rpm, then shifted up into fifth, still accelerating toward that magic number of the dial.

It ran like the wind. *I* ran like the wind. It was as though I became the car, or the car became me, and which was which didn't matter anymore. Road, driver, and machine were blended into a single entity, an unholy union of asphalt and steel and flesh. Blood pounded through my veins and the tires pounded on the pavement until the pulses fused and became simply the pulse of movement.

And all the time, I was vaguely aware of a half-smile hovering around my mouth. It was a smile of intense joy and satisfaction, kept in check by the concentration demanded by the speed, yet undeniably there.

The daemon had emerged, and demanded recognition. Not the demon of medieval imagination, with horns and tail, but the *daemon* of the ancient Greeks, that pure-burning flame that could take over and hold humans in its grasp, burn them up in its service, inspire and consume them at the same time. Both a curse and a blessing, it was the genie behind the genius. There was something in it of fate, as fickle-fingered as ever, with the potential for both good and evil. Or, as Nietzsche would have it, the potential to go beyond good and evil.

In the 911, I felt as though I had entered a new world: a metaphysics of speed. I didn't care how long the trip took, or even where I was going. All that mattered was the driving itself. I seemed to exist beyond time, in the absolute moment. On that clear, curving highway, everything else disappeared. There was just me and the car and the road, and nothing else in all of God's existence.

When I reached my journey's end, all I wanted was to do it again. And across the expanse of the years and miles that have intervened since then, I am still trying to figure out exactly what happened at the precise moment when I recognized the daemon.

I will try to be honest here. As honest as the daemon will allow. It still has me in its grip, but I am battling it now, and I know that to succeed, I must first understand it. Perhaps, as a writer, I place too much faith in catharsis—in the idea that by describing and exploring the obsession with speed that began that fine spring day in Vermont, I can drive it out of me.

The trouble is, I'm still not sure if I really want to do that. The daemon clearly still has the upper hand. And although the socially responsible side of me, the side I always thought of as my real self, abhors the effect this has on my mind, the danger I present to others and to myself on the road, the amount of burnt oil I contribute to the pollution of this planet—it is no use. Put me behind the wheel of a fast car, and speed takes over.

This is not just my personal problem. It is also a political one. On a personal level, I cannot escape the hold speed has on me until I understand it. On the political level, none of us can.

At the end of the twentieth century, we are still using a one-hundred-year-old technology: the internal-combustion engine. And this basic piece of mechanics pollutes the air so badly that in Los Angeles white air-filters turn black within twenty-four hours, while there are days in Mexico City when people's noses bleed and birds fall dead out of the sky. Yet there is no doubt in my mind that my new-found delight in speed was intimately bound up with the atavistic qualities of the internal-combustion engine: the vibration and the roar of it, the burning heat, that sense of live metal. And it seems to me that until we can understand the hold of internal combustion over our imaginations and our lives, we cannot achieve a sane balance between our desire for mobility and our desire for a livable planet. One way or another, we are all in thrall to the daemon.

The problem runs far deeper than reason or common sense. After all, I should have been one of the last people to be entranced by speed. I had always thought of cars primarily as a convenience—a way of getting from point A to point B in relative safety and ease. At least, that's the way I liked to think I thought of them. And as the data on the greenhouse effect and automobile emissions became clearer and more precise, I became almost anti-car. I felt it was pointless to build cars that could go two or three or even four times the speed limit: irresponsible at the very least, criminally negligent at the worst. Such cars, I thought, merely catered to the worst aspects of teenage macho.

So what was I doing, a woman in her early forties, discovering the transcendent joys of the internal-combustion engine? Where were my principles? My integrity? What was happening to me?

On one level, what happened was quite mundane. By chance, I had begun to write a monthly column about cars. This began with a flip remark on a revolving dance floor—the one in the Rainbow Room at the top of New York's Rockefeller Center, which had just reopened. The occasion was a party to launch a new magazine for which I was a contributing editor, and the supply of champagne was lavish. I was aware of being somewhat drunk when, after the stranger I was dancing with told me that he was the area representative for Range Rover, I batted my eyelashes and heard myself saying, "Do you realize that a Range Rover is every Englishman's wet dream?"

The upshot was that two weeks later, I was the possessor of a Range Rover for one week, with the mission of testing it and writing a piece about it. One car led to another, and before I quite realized what was happening, the column existed. It was called "Carnal Knowledge."

It seemed a harmless, temporary change of interest at first. After years of working as a political journalist, I felt as though I were riding the froth of the wave instead of struggling with the undertow. I insisted, of course, that this newfound interest was not worth taking seriously. "Just a passing fancy," I'd say to friends. "We'll see if it lasts three months." Then, "Let's see if it lasts another three months." Then, "Maybe a year." And then I stopped talking about how long it would last.

I stopped when it was clear that I was utterly hooked. But I suspect I already knew that when I hit 130 miles an hour in the Porsche, because what happened at that moment was like an injection of some wonderful new drug. In that moment, I discovered that speed can possess you. It takes over all your senses. There is the tunnel vision of sight; the massive orchestra of the engine in your ears; the smell of copious amounts of oil burning; the vibration through the wheel, delivering the feel of the road itself literally into your hands. And yes, even the taste of it—a taste that rises onto the top of your palate from somewhere deep inside you, a taste not unlike sweet Belon oysters, perhaps. It is, I think, the pure, unadulterated taste of adrenaline.

I was to drive faster cars, at faster speeds, but the 911 was the one that introduced me to the many levels of transgression inherent in speed, and therefore still embodies them in my mind. There was something about it that recognized neither morality nor common sense. The only laws it seemed to acknowledge were those of physics, and sometimes it was as though it could annihilate those too. This car could almost make possible the impossible. In it, I imagined I could fly.

I know that I am in a double bind here. Even as I try to understand speed, I cannot help but romanticize it. I make it glamorous by the apparently simple act of trying to describe it. For transgression often holds an aura of glamour. And therefore of seductiveness.

Transgression is inherent in the very idea of transport, from the humdrum of the Transportation Authority to the heights of transports of ecstasy. It is built into the word. *Trans:* the Latin for "across" or "beyond." *Port:* from the Latin for "to carry." Something that carries you across. Across space. Across time. Across boundaries.

Make the word transgression instead of transport, and you add in the intentionality of the Latin *gradi*—to move or step. Transgression is thus a deliberate challenge of boundaries.

French philosopher Michel Foucault saw it as "the interrogation of boundaries." And breaking through them, he wrote, "affords an exhilarating sense of freedom."

That too was part of what I experienced at speed that day in Vermont. And I would come to realize that although I may have been as surprised as anyone else when I began to write about cars, I had stumbled on a perfect subject, precisely because transgression was inherent in it: for me as a woman entering a stereotypically male field of interest; for me as a writer concerned with political and environmental issues; for me as a law-abiding citizen suddenly taking great delight in flouting the law. In fact, as a friend pointed out, one way or another I had been living on and crossing boundaries for years.

Whether physical or psychological, a boundary has always seemed to me something that invites testing. I'm not sure if this is sheer orneriness on my part, or journalistic curiosity, or some existential fate in life that keeps me eternally on the alert. But there is no doubt that at that particular point in time, for someone who had lived on three continents, who was on her way to her third citizenship, and who sometimes talked of having had three lives "so far," cars were an ideal outlet for the need for movement and transgression.

Certainly, cars had always represented escape for me: escape from where I was, and escape toward something new, unknown. They were a release from stasis. They were the means of voyaging, of achieving a sense of travel and adventure. And always, they could take you beyond yourself.

Every teenager knows this. Everyone who remembers what it was like to put your foot down on the throttle for the first time and feel the car move. There was that thrill—that moment of amazement, that sudden surge of excitement, and that sense, however fleeting, of having somehow crossed a line, of having stepped not just down on the throttle, but beyond adolescence and into adulthood, into a realm where you could move farther and faster than ever before. It was empowerment, and it was intoxicating.

Up there in northern Vermont, with the highway as clear as the sky, I rode the surface of the earth in the Porsche, dipping and curving with the land itself. I felt as though I owned the road, as though I had somehow made it mine. And soon the steeply sloped hood created a strange illusion: the road became a ribbon disappearing straight into the car as the engine rolled up the asphalt and devoured it.

Seen in quick glances in the rearview mirror, the road behind was in rapid-fire disappearance, like in a speeded-up movie. After a while, it seemed, there *was* no road behind me. It became not a road but a wilderness, a vacuum, a vast emptiness that had no meaning or relevance or reality. *Après moi le déluge*. There was no room in my consciousness for it. Only what was ahead existed. And because I was traveling so fast, the future became the present. In fact, there *was* no future. And no past. Speed became an annihilation of time.

Jean Baudrillard, fascinated like so many French intellectuals by the American road culture, called speed "an amnesiac intoxication . . . . It is itself a pure object, since it cancels out the ground and territorial reference points . . . . Its only rule is to leave no trace behind. It is the triumph of forgetting over memory."

The result is almost a kind of meditation. I realize only afterward that driving fast is tiring. That I am, in fact, exhausted. For as long as it lasts, I am totally alert, in and of the moment, both that particular moment and the coming moments of the next quarter or half mile. I am emptied out of all else. My life does not exist. My problems have vanished. It is almost as though I myself do not exist. In some strange way, even as I feel myself absolutely alive—heart beating hard, brain in constant calculation, muscles straining in my back, my neck, my arms, my legs—I cease to exist. Paradoxically, in absolute existence there *is* no existence—none of that ongoing process of existence that is our experience of life.

Nihilistic as this is, it feels wonderful. But how did this go together with my socially responsible self? If I had touched the transcendent headiness of speed for the first time, I had also caught my first glimpse of how darkly antisocial it can be. In both the light and the darkness, I recognized the daemon. And I knew that, by its nature, it was not going to quietly slip back to whatever deep regions of my mind it had emerged from. The only way to deal with the daemon, I resolved, was to explore it further. If I could enter into the essence of speed, perhaps I could emerge the other side purged, with some newfound sense of sanity. Perhaps, after all, catharsis could work.

This exploration would become an ongoing journey. En route, I would work as a mechanic's apprentice, in the hope that by understanding how cars worked—by getting right into the belly of the beast, as it were—I could grasp some further dimension of our almost hypnotic subservience to the internal-combustion engine. The journey would also lead me into certain dark spaces of the mind that few people mention publicly when they talk about speed, although I know from quiet, unguarded one-on-one discussions that many experience it. And eventually, it would lead me to the perfect irony that I had discovered the transcendent delights of the internal-combustion engine just as it was nearing the end of its era.

All this, however, would come later. First, I would have to find out just how fast I could go.

II

A UNIVERSITY OF PENNSYLVANIA PSYCHOLOGIST named Richard Solomon has developed something called "the opponent-process theory." It says, in essence, that an extreme experience will produce the opposite sensation, in much the same way, perhaps, that staring at a red circle will produce a halo in the complementary color, green.

I like this theory. It makes me feel normal. How else explain that from such terror as I experienced my first time on a racetrack, I could develop such elation?

I was at Lime Rock Park, a winding 2.3-mile track surrounded by the woods and gentle hills of northeastern

Connecticut. Lime Rock is Paul Newman's favorite track; he has won a few races there. But on this particular day, such information made no impression on me. Even if Newman had been in the pits, I doubt that my fear would have allowed me to so much as register his presence. This was the first day of the Skip Barber competition racing school, and all I wanted to do was pack my things back into the rental car with the fading brakes and the misaligned front left wheel and go home.

The moment I'd gotten a close-up look at the open-wheel Formula Ford that they told me I'd be driving for the next three days, my mouth had gone dry. The flexible fiberglass body seemed horribly insubstantial. The suspension struts stuck out nakedly, thin bars that seemed to stretch forever to the wheels. The engine looked raw, basic, with no attempt to soothe a consumer's eye as in what I would soon learn to call "street cars." The whole thing seemed terrifyingly small and frail. Elemental.

There was a plain plastic molded seat with no padding, a tiny steering wheel, and a shift so tight and cramped that the only way you could change gears was by backhanding it. In front of the wheel was a tachometer, an oil gauge, a temperature gauge, and an ignition switch. That was it. Not even a speedometer.

"You want me to drive *this?*" I wanted to say. Instead, I swallowed hard. I'd do a lot of swallowing hard in those three days. But as the only woman in a group of twelve students, I was damned if I'd be the one to bail out. Whether you call that feminist macho or simple pride, the effect was the same: I drove through my terror.

It took a day and a half until I reached the moment of breakthrough. I was just coming out of the big bend and into the ess bend, with the tachometer nudging 6,000 rpm, and it was a toss-up as to which was shaking harder, the car or me. Every slightest rise in what had at first seemed the smoothest of pavements now felt like a huge bump, and my helmet was banging against the roll cage. Oddly, inside the helmet, I found that a very comforting sound.

I was trying to concentrate on what my instructor, Bruce MacInnes, had told me. "As I understand it," I'd said, "you want me to come full throttle into the ess, pointed diagonally away from the direction of the curve. And somewhere past the last possible rational moment, you want me to threshold brake—brake to the point just before the wheels lock up. And then, still braking, you want me to turn the wheel about two inches in the direction of the bend."

He smiled affably. For some reason, I suddenly registered how very blue his eyes were. "That's it," he said.

"The only trouble with all that is that it runs counter to some peculiar instinct in me," I replied. "I think it's called a survival instinct."

He gave a wide grin of agreement. "To drive well," he said, "you have to override your instinct."

There was nothing to do but swallow hard again.

"Have faith!" he shouted as I put my helmet on and got back into the car. "Trust what we tell you. Remember: Hebrews eleven, verse one!"

I'd never heard of Hebrews eleven, verse one, until Bruce kept telling me to remember it. The night before, I'd looked it up, courtesy of the Gideons, in the Bible beside my hotel bed: "Faith is the substance of things hoped for, the evidence of things not seen."

This was not comforting.

But the next day, obedient to the biblical command, I took a deep breath, charged out of the pits, changed up into third as I came out of the big bend, and went full down on the throttle. The car roared down toward the ess bend. I saw the tree the other side of the track looming large right in front of me, heard the vroom-vroom as I double declutched, felt the force of deceleration as I braked down to the threshold, and turned the wheel two inches to the left.

And then it happened: My eyes opened wider than they'd ever been before as I heard the tires screaming even above the roar of the motor and the whole car went into a controlled slide, rotating round the bend high on the rim as though it were cornering all by itself, with only the minimum effort from me to keep it on course. As it began to point into the apex of the second part of the ess, I eased off the brakes and back onto the throttle and went roaring through the rest of the curve, punching the air with my right fist and shouting in pure delight until I was off down the back straight with a grin on my face that had to be wider than the track.

The way I felt right then, I might as well have just won Le Mans.

The absence of a speedometer bothered me at first. Every time I came into the pits, I'd ask what speed I'd been doing, and Bruce would smilingly oblige. It took some time for me to grasp that raw speed was not the measure on the racetrack, no matter the obsession with it of onlookers and television commentators. The real measure was time. How fast you went was a matter not of miles per hour but of seconds and tenths of seconds per lap. The speedometer was irrelevant. Only the stopwatch mattered.

The exhilaration of speed, I would discover, cannot be expressed by a simple figure on the speedometer. Raw speed is a one-time sensation, not an experience. It becomes far more complex, and therefore far more interesting, when you learn to handle a fast car, when you begin to prefer the corners to the straights.

"Any fool can drive fast in a straight line," said Mike Zimicki, my second instructor at Lime Rock. "What they don't realize is that driving a race car is a matter of the mind, not muscle. It's like playing chess at two hundred miles an hour."

Driving helter-skelter at speed is merely reckless. Driving in control at speed is something else. And driving at the edge of control—pushing car and driver to the limit—is a matter of high skill, of perfect coordination between muscle, eye, and brain, and between car, road, and driver. To do it, you need far more than mere guts or nerve. You need an intimate understanding of dynamics, of what happens to metal, rubber, and air under strong acceleration and braking.

This extraordinary blending of human and machine can be so fine that it is measurable, if at all, in millimeters. "You need to refine your foot movement on the pedal," Mike told me as I was practicing threshold braking in the infield. "Don't move your leg. Don't even move your foot. Just flex your foot inside your shoe."

"Maybe I should just *think* about moving my foot," I said in as sardonic a tone as I could muster.

"That would work," he replied, straight-faced.

And it did. Just a tensing of the foot eased or applied enough pressure on the brake pedal to bring me to the absolute threshold of lock-up, with the maximum braking power. Not one millimeter over, when I'd have locked the wheels and spun, nor one under, when I wouldn't have had enough braking power to take the corner fast.

At Lime Rock, in short, I learned to drive fast with finesse. Mike would say that I learned to play chess. Bruce that I learned the evidence of things not seen. I would say that I learned to dance.

I'd been up in Saratoga Springs a month or so before, while the New York City Ballet was summering there. Mid-mornings, I'd take a bicycle and ride on down to the amphitheater to watch the company in rehearsal. There was something infinitely more satisfying in watching the dancers then, in sweatpants and leggings, ragged tops and vests, than in seeing the formal perfection of the evening performances. I could see their muscles trembling under the tension, the concentration on their faces, the sweat stains on their clothes. I could see both the effort and the perfection of the result, the two coexistent, without the illusion of effortlessness created by lights and makeup. This way, it seemed both more real and more miraculous. I was watching everything in the dancers' bodies strain to create perfect form, and the strain was *part* of the form. If truly effortless, it would not have held my interest.

And now it occurred to me, at Lime Rock, that there is a similar grace in taking a car fast around curves and bends, having it hold the road at its limit. On the track as on the stage, there is such a thing as perfect form.

There is, in fact, a perfect line around the track—the racing line, they call it. It has no necessary relation to the shortest line. It is the line that will move you fastest if you know how to corner, the line that will use every bit of momentum inherent not only in the car but in the track itself. And to drive this line requires perfect rhythm: the basic rhythm of gears and pedals and wheels onto which the driver plays the tune of the particular track or road. Played well—driven well—it is perfect harmony.

The poet Czeslaw Milosz called it "that unified trinity: I, motor, Earth." It is perhaps the ultimate blending of human and machine. Both intention and effort are at such a peak that mind and body transcend them and enter a zone of perfection—the sweet zone that athletes talk about—in which you are no longer conscious of intention or effort, and performance itself is all.

Mike Zimicki was right again. In those three days at Lime Rock, I discovered a delight that was both intensely physical and yet intensely intellectual too. It seemed that with good focus, good skill, and a measure of good fortune, I could enter at will into the pure realm that is the experience of the absolute essence of speed. Speed seemed to become a state of mind, even a state of being. You become speed. You are speed. You do have wings.

And for such illusions, of course, there is a price to pay.

III

A RACE CAR IS A MACHINE in which to tempt fate: to dare it, to challenge it, and—as I learned at Lime Rock—to overcome it. But for the first couple of days in that tiny open-wheel Formula Ford, the shadow of Icarus seemed to shimmer above my head whenever I took the time to stand still and think. The only way to shake him off was in movement, until, like him, I gained that novice's illusion of perfect control.

The penalties for speed are harsh. But sometimes it seems they are less for speed itself than for the hubris with which we presume to go faster than we were designed to. Perhaps that is why we so admire race drivers: they dare the fates.

And the fates, challenged, sometimes answer in kind. Why else did Icarus die?

There he is, a teenager living on Crete together with his father, Daedalus, who is a mechanical genius and the designer of the famed labyrinth. You would think King Minos would decorate and honor him for this, but kings are jealous creatures, and instead Minos imprisons Daedalus and his son in a tower, to prevent anyone else from having access to the secret of the labyrinth. Dictators have always been shortsighted, preferring to enforce loyalty than to evoke it.

A prison tower is no great impediment to an inventor of Daedalus' level. He and Icarus escape, but they are still trapped on the island of Crete, and Minos' secret police have all the ports under surveillance. So Daedalus invents what is essentially the first airplane. He makes wings for himself and his son. He uses the feathers of real birds, molds them with wax into two huge skeletal structures with backstraps, and then, like an eagle in her aerie, teaches his son how to fly. And when the time has come for the flight overseas, he tells Icarus: "Fly neither too high nor too low. If you fly too low, the damp from the earth's surface will clog your wings, make them heavy, and bring you down to earth. If you fly too high, the heat of the sun will melt the wax and your wings will disintegrate. Keep to a moderate height. Follow me."

Did he forget that he was talking to a teenager?

They fly away from the island of Crete, the first men ever to fly, and with the vast expanse of the Aegean Sea below him, Icarus begins to exult in this extraordinary freedom.

21

He starts to experiment, to swoop and soar. He does figures of eight and looping rolls, and the more he does, the more confidence he gains. He laughs with the sheer pleasure of it, flexes his wings, and soars even higher because the sun is there, high up in the heavens, and if he flies high enough he can reach the sun and be free of earth.

He flies so high that he is way out of reach of his father's warning voice, and all the warnings he has had before become just vague memories as though from another life long discarded. The higher he goes, the more luminous the light and the purer the air. The height is so exhilarating that he is convinced that nothing can stop him now, that he is immortal....

And then the inevitable happens. The heat of the sun begins to melt the wax of his wings. One by one, the feathers come loose, and as they drop off, Icarus loses his balance, that perfect grace of flight that had him so entranced. He pitches and yaws, and still the wax melts, and still the feathers fall. He flaps his arms, and nothing happens because his wings now are full of holes. And then finally, still struggling for impossible control, he falls, a tiny figure tumbling out of the sky, pitching over and over, round and round, what is left of his wings tangled around his body as he plunges into the depths of the sea.

Only one person sees him fall. Daedalus is the only one to witness all that remains of his son: a few feathers floating on the surface of the Aegean Sea. The gods allowed Daedalus his genius, but only to be used in moderation. For those immoderate—for those who would go beyond the limits of the human in an attempt to be as gods—they exact their vengeance.

Whenever I drive fast, there is always a shade of awareness that somehow, in some manner, I am in transgression of the laws of nature. That is, of the normal boundaries of physical life. I am moving faster than my body is designed to move.

The fastest you can move without mechanical aid is about fifteen miles an hour, and only the best runners can do that. The fastest you can move with mechanical aid is supersonic, but unless you are a pilot, your experience of that is entirely passive, as a passenger in an aluminum tube with no real sense of speed. The fastest you can go and really *feel* it actively—in your whole body—is in a car.

Driving fast is intensely physical. Even in normal, everyday driving, you use not only your hands on the wheel but also your feet on the pedals, your eyes on the road and the mirrors, and your brain processing everything.

Most good drivers are aware of this much. Your back, your neck, and your shoulders are in constant tension. So are your arms and your hands. Even your backside, responsive to the vibration of rubber on asphalt rising literally through the seat of your pants, feeds information to your brain.

"Acceleration," auto journalist John Jerome once wrote, "is one of the most massive sensory experiences we ever have. It is a sensory intensifier." When everything is working superbly, body seems to meld with machine, muscle with steel, as though the steel too had intelligence, and the body the power of metal. But the real sense of physical transgression doesn't happen until you experience the g-force—the

23

push of acceleration, the rising curve, the pressure of physics against flesh.

The g-force is essentially dislocation. Being moved out of place. The human body's place on this earth is at a certain speed, at a certain angle. The balance mechanism of the inner ear helps see to that, as do the eyes, and the whole body musculature. And, of course, gravity. But at speed, especially around corners or in sudden acceleration, centrifugal force takes over. There is no doubt that this force is outside you, and is stronger than you. It works on you with such pressure that it seems as though your body is moved first and your insides follow after. You are pushed back hard into the seat in acceleration, and pulled to the right or the left in hard cornering. Your neck, shoulders, and back tense as you struggle to keep your eyes level. You are, literally, thrown at an angle to the world.

Most of us know this sensation from the fairground ride—the roller coaster or the cyclone—but there we are entirely passive. When we drive hard, however, it is as though we ourselves create this force. We can produce it at will.

Race drivers contend with g-forces so great that they are subject to three or four times the normal force of gravity. From a standing start, a Formula One car will reach a hundred miles an hour in just under three seconds. And in that first second, the driver's head is pushed back so violently that his face distends, giving him a ghostly smile.

Within another second, he has changed gears twice, and each time he does so, the acceleration force smashes him back into the seat again. After three seconds, accelerating upward from a hundred miles an hour toward two hundred, his peripheral vision is completely blurred. He can only see straight ahead. The eight-hundred-horsepower engine is screaming at 130 decibels, and each piston completes four combustion cycles ten thousand times a minute, which means that the vibration he feels is at that rate.

His neck and shoulder muscles are under immense strain, trying to keep his eyes level as the g-force pushes his head from side to side in the corners. The strong acceleration makes blood pool in his legs so that less is delivered to the heart, which means that there's less cardiac output, forcing the pulse rate up. Formula One drivers' pulses are often up to 180, even 200, and they stay at eighty-five percent of that maximum for almost the entire length of a two-hour race.

More: Breathing quickens as the muscles call for more blood—speed literally takes your breath away—and the whole body goes into emergency stance. A two-hour emergency. The mouth goes dry, the eyes dilate as the car travels the length of a football field for every normal heartbeat. The brain processes information at an astonishingly rapid rate, since the higher the speed, the less the reaction time. Moreover, reactions have to be not only quick but also extraordinarily precise, no matter how great the physical strain. Split seconds may be mere slivers of time, but they are also the difference between winning and losing a race, or between entering and avoiding a crash.

In short, a Formula One driver has to be almost preternaturally alert under conditions of maximum physical pressure. Obviously, the adrenaline is pumping, helping the body cope with this intensity of sensation and information. Everything is primed for instantaneity. The driver has to be in top physical condition. But in addition to the physical fitness of top athletes, he also needs that chess player's mind as he assimilates telemetry data, calculates overtaking points, and executes a racing strategy. All of which is why speed is so dangerous for most of us: we simply have neither the physical nor the mental stamina to handle it.

Psychologically, what happens in a race is still more complex. The muscles, the brain chemicals, the laws of physics, the vibration, the conditions of the race—all these combine to generate a high level of excitement and tension in the body, making the driver feel absolutely, totally clearheaded and alert. And high.

I once asked Emerson Fittipaldi if he still found speed exciting. After two Formula One World Championships and an Indianapolis 500 win, I imagined that somehow he'd be used to it. Both body and mind must adapt, I thought, so that the extraordinary finally becomes ordinary. But on the contrary. A faraway look came into Fittipaldi's eyes as he talked about being in a race, as though he were running the track again right there, in his mind. His mouth and hands seemed to search for the words to name the ineffable.

"When I come into the first turn at Indianapolis at two hundred and thirty-five miles an hour with the car in perfect balance," he said finally, "it is absolutely thrilling. There is nothing like it in the world." The sensual force of it was palpable in his voice. He paused, staring off into the distance of the track in his mind, eyes soft and dreamy. "If I ever lose that thrill," he added quietly, "I'll stop racing."

And he went on to talk of the physical limits inherent in racing, limits established by the human body, by mechanical engineering, and by the track itself. These limits were the challenge, and yet clearly also the goal. The idea of unlimited speed held no fascination for him. "Driving without limits would not be interesting," he mused. It was as though he needed them to provoke him and urge him on. His aim is to be at the outer limit. Beyond that, he knows, is to be dead.

This sense of limits is what keeps Fittipaldi mortal. It is also what keeps him alive. For those of us far less experienced in dealing with speed, there is a dangerous illusion of being beyond the limits—of being godlike, or immortal. That is the high, and that is a deeper level of transgression.

Perhaps Phaeton is a better example than Icarus. Especially since his name was borrowed, presumably in ignorance of his fate, for the early touring cars. After all, Icarus wanted only to reach the sun. Phaeton wants to *be* the sun.

He is one of those unfortunates who are the offspring of a god and a human—in his case, the sun god Apollo and the nymph Clymene. Reaching adolescence, the boy begins to question his absent father's reality, so his mother sends him east, to where the sun rises, to his father's palace. Apollo welcomes him fulsomely, and as absentee fathers tend to do, promises his young son anything in the world to prove his fatherly love for him.

Phaeton is a teenager. What does his father think he'll ask for? He asks, of course, to drive the chariot of the sun for one day.

Apollo tries to dissuade his son. "Your lot is mortal, and you ask what is beyond a mortal's power," he says. But Phaeton is still the son of a god and is not to be deterred.

All that Apollo can do is warn him of the danger points on the route:

"The first part of the way is steep, and such as the horses when fresh in the morning can hardly climb; the middle is high up in the heavens, whence I myself can scarcely, without alarm, look down and behold the earth and sea stretched below me. The last part of the road descends rapidly, and requires most careful driving. Tethys, who is waiting to receive me, often trembles for me lest I should fall headlong. Added to all this, the heaven is all the time turning round and carrying the stars with it. I have to be perpetually on my guard lest that movement, which sweeps everything else along, should hurry me also away. . . . Nor will you find it easy to guide these horses, with their breasts full of fire that they breathe forth from their mouths and nostrils. I can scarcely govern them myself, when they are unruly and resist the reins."

Any race driver will recognize this description of the course. And the race car.

When Phaeton still insists, Apollo sighs and gives him one last piece of advice: "The horses go fast enough of their own accord; the labor is to hold them in. Avoid the northern and the southern ways; go not too high, or you will burn the heavenly dwellings, nor too low, or you will set the earth on fire; go most safely in the middle." Almost exactly what Daedalus told Icarus.

No self-respecting teenager, of course, has any intention of keeping safely to the middle. Not that Phaeton will even have a chance to try. The minute the horses are given the rein, they sense the lighter load, know they are free of control, and go dashing madly about the heavens as Phaeton hangs on for dear life in the chariot behind them, shaking in terror. The heavens are scorched; the earth is scorched. And finally both heaven and earth call on Zeus, the ruler of the gods, to stop this torture. Zeus gathers his famous lightning bolts and hurls them one after another against Phaeton. The boy is struck from the chariot and falls head-long back toward the earth, his hair on fire, like a shooting star.

You would think that this is a simple enough parable about the dangers of reaching too far and too high, but the ancient Greeks were far from simplistic. The story has an epilogue. Once Phaeton's body has fallen to earth, the beautiful Nayads erect a tombstone for him, with these words: "He could not rule his father's car of fire. Yet was it much so nobly to aspire."

In life, Phaeton was an ambitious, stupid teenager. But in death, despite the damage he caused both heaven and earth, he becomes a hero for daring the impossible.

It is only fitting that the greater the transgression, the more dramatic the punishment. But there seems to be some human need for a further step: the more dramatic the punishment, the greater the heroism ascribed. Icarus merely overreaches and falls to a watery grave in lonely isolation. Phaeton aspires to take the place of the gods—not just to be like a god, but to *be* one—and is honored for his failure.

Would James Dean's legend be quite so great if he had merely caught pneumonia instead of crashing his Porsche

Spyder race car on a country road? Would we think differently of Isadora Duncan if she had died in her sleep instead of tangling her long scarf in the wheel spokes of her Rolls Royce Corniche and strangling to death? Both died in motion, at speed, in fast cars, and their deaths became part of their legends. The style of death acted as a fitting coda to their lives, which had been spent pushing the limits, going for broke, each in his or her own way.

I've heard it said that Jack Kerouac *should* have died on the road, in a car crash, long before his drawn-out decline into alcoholic torpor. Maybe it is so with any figure who shines bright in the sky of our cultural pantheon, who seems to burn up with his or her energy and sets our imaginations on fire. We want the drama of the fiery, dramatic end for them. We ignore the reality of mangled steel and flesh, arms and legs akimbo and skull caved in, scorched and disfigured flesh studded with shards of glass and fragments of steel. As we romanticize and glamorize the motion itself, so too we gild its abrupt end.

A hero is someone who defies death—or at least mortality, figuratively speaking. Someone who reaches beyond the boundaries of everydayness and explores a further realm. Someone who defies normality. And sometimes, inevitably, that defiance will be too mocking. The hero overreaches, or there'll be a slip of judgment, or that fickle finger of fate will come into play like a *deus ex machina* that seems written into the scenario of the hero's life beforehand: a wayward scarf, or a truck out of control, or a farmer daydreaming in his pickup. Death wins and claims the body. But not the legend. Death merely makes the legend larger.

Are we, to some extent, trying to make our lives legendary when we speed? Certainly we add drama and excitement to them, both in our own eyes and in the eyes of others. And part of that is the glamour not of speed itself but of daring death.

"Life is impoverished, it loses in interest, when the highest stake in the game, life itself, may not be risked." So wrote Sigmund Freud in his essay "Thoughts for the Times on War and Death." Like war, speed carries the possibility of death. It tantalizes it, teases it, almost tempts it. And this is part of what makes speed so seductive. In the act of defying death, the whole body is indubitably alive, full of vitality, and the contrast arouses us.

The death defied lacks reality. We think we will go out, if at all, in a blaze of light. We try not to consider the far likelier outcome of paraplegia. Death enters the realm of legend, of heroes and stars. It is mythic. And playing with it can therefore be erotic.

Eros and Thanatos—Freud's twin poles of desire, separate and yet intertwined—play off and against each other as the lodestars in our lives. And on the road. Driving at speed becomes an extraordinary combination of polar opposites: beauty and terror, intention and spontaneity, imagination and pragmatism, excitement and deliberation, intellect and atavistic physical response. And sometimes, with the whole body under intense stimulation, speed crosses another boundary, goes beyond the sensuous and even the sensual, and becomes sexual.

It happened to me in the Porsche 911. I could say it was merely the vibration through the seat and the wheel, the general physical arousal, the high level of endorphins. I could put it down to all these things, and yet I know I would be lying.

After all, what would any daemon be without a sexual component?

I am not talking about sex as a metaphor. I am talking about direct, physical sexual arousal behind the wheel of a powerful car at speed. It happened to me that once, and it was unmistakable—the tug in my lower abdomen, the warm, melting sensation spreading out from there, that feeling of losing all boundaries between my body and the world. Even as it was happening, as the force of acceleration pulled me back against the seat and the vibration of the car seemed to become my own, I felt that I was riding that thin fine line between control and absolute surrender of control, and some part of me, that part of me that had always existed long before I even knew what a Porsche 911 looked like, managed somehow to struggle to the surface and say, "Slow down, for Christ's sake slow down." And as I did so, the arousal died down in me, and I was once again a rational, sentient being behind the wheel of a machine, left with the sobering realization that the familiar and hackneyed sexual symbolism of the car derives not from imagination but from experience.

Can I say it was the daemon, or is that just an excuse? After all, there are those who consider sex itself to be daemonic. "In the day we are social creatures," wrote cultural critic Camille Paglia in her book *Sexual Personae*, "but at night we descend to the dream world where nature reigns, where there is no law but sex, cruelty, and metamorphosis. Day itself is invaded by daemonic night. Moment by moment, night flickers in the imagination, in eroticism, subverting our strivings for virtue and order."

She has a strong point: Speed is profoundly erotic not only in and of itself but also because it is subversive. The daemon thrives on the many levels of transgression involved. And it now becomes clear that, as a woman, the very subject of cars is itself a form of transgression for me. And this, of course, is an essential part of my attraction to them.

IV

IT WAS A LOVELY, ALMOST ENCHANTED EVENING—fittingly, since we were gathered on the terrace of the Enchantment Resort in Sedona, Arizona, some dozen automotive journalists who had spent the day test-driving the next year's cars. The red-rock canyon glowed in the dying light. We sipped champagne, I tossed my head to show off my new cloisonné cactus earrings, someone said what wonderful perfume I was wearing.

We were chatting pleasantly in a tight little group. These automotive journalists are, for the most part, gentle, mild-mannered men, and I have learned a lot from them. Most have been involved with cars all their working lives. They've driven every car you can name, they collect vintage cars, and some even race their own cars.

I forget exactly what we were talking about—it was certainly something to do with cars—when in the distance we heard the sound of a powerful sports car coming up the long drive. The deep throb of the engine reverberated off the canyon walls, and although we kept talking, an element of unreality crept into the conversation as inner eyes focused on that unseen car.

As it approached, the sound grew thicker, and conversation seemed to slow, almost to halt. And then, just below where we were standing, the driver dropped the clutch. The exhaust gave a deep-throated roar that echoed up and down the canyon, there was a flash of red metal, and instantly, as though in instinctive response to some mysterious call of the wild, the men turned and started walking toward that sound.

I followed after. I could hear the car going up to the top of the drive, turning, coming back. Then finally it came into view, pulled off onto the lawn, and stopped right in front of us: the sole prototype of the Dodge Viper, the aggressively styled V-10 muscle car that had been a fixture in Detroit rumor for months. There had been photographs of it in the automotive press, but nobody outside a small design group and the heads of Chrysler had yet seen it "in the flesh."

The men gathered around it admiringly. Suddenly, they seemed more like teenage boys than knowledgeable journalists. But what followed next took me even more by surprise. One by one, they asked if they could sit in the driver's seat. Each strapped himself in, grasped the wheel, and asked for his photograph to be taken.

What entranced them was not the feel of four hundred horsepower capable of two hundred miles an hour, since the design chief, who'd done the fancy driving, was keeping the keys deep in his pocket; he had no intention of submitting his sole prototype to any uncontrolled real-world testing. There was no doubt that the magic lay in their imaginations. It was the mystique of pure, raw power.

By now I'm used to the eager enthusiasm of the sons of friends, to whom I give the posters of exotic supercars sent me by automakers. The boys pin them up on their walls, and ask me questions focused exclusively on engine size and horsepower and speed. But these were grown men. Men I liked and respected, with a highly sophisticated knowledge of cars. Yet a single throb of the exhaust, tuned to the deep reverberation of power, had been enough to send them back to awestruck enchantment.

Finally, I too sat behind the wheel. As I'd expected, I got no thrill from it. No frisson of power. I was far more interested in clambering over the mesas to watch the sun set than in inanimate metal. If I'd gotten hold of the keys, that would have been different. The car would have burst into motion. I could have combined setting sun and hot metal, speeding off into the sunset in a flash of red and a pulse of sound. But that wasn't to be that evening.

Someone took my picture. I shrugged, unhooked the racing harness, and climbed out. I dutifully looked at the engine, as everyone else had done. Big. Powerful. Raw. It was handmade, which I found the most interesting thing about it. The designers boasted that this was a car designed specifically to evoke the old muscle cars of the 1960s. A car that practically snubbed its nose at the latest technology and went instead for raw power. But I just didn't get it.

I knew part of the reason: I didn't have the past with cars that these men had. I was coming to an intimate knowledge of cars in my forties; they had come to it as teenagers. This means that with the one exception of my first long-gone car, a Citroën Deux Chevaux, I have no nostalgia for cars, no automobile adventures that somehow seem to encapsulate the feeling of another time. For most American men, a muscle car is youth and freedom. For me, it is an anachronism.

"What's the point?" I wanted to ask, but I didn't. You don't ask for the point of nostalgia. For the point of youth.

I felt very sane and female that evening in Sedona, and that surprised me.

I thought by then I had entered the world where cars exert their own charisma. I imagined I had already crossed the boundary and committed the transgression of gender, of being a woman in what is stereotypically thought of as a man's world.

The delight of transgression lies as much in the act of committing it as in the content of it. But the content has its own satisfaction. There are good reasons why, as long as I can remember, I seem to have had this macho streak in me.

I'm not sure where it came from. Rebelliousness, perhaps. Something as simple as being a tomboy when I was a child, although God knows I was terrified of climbing trees, and had to force myself to do it just to preserve my reputation. That, of course—not the fact of climbing trees, but doing it despite myself—was the real macho part of it.

I do know that I confound psychological wisdom in that this streak has become stronger as I've grown older. It shows in ways I don't intend: in my style of playing ping-pong or a pool game, going for the dramatic shots even if it means losing points, or in my stubbornness over certain issues. "You think like a man!" one of my women friends complained when I pointed out that there were more productive things to do than think about relationships all the time.

Her accusation disturbs me. It reminds me of a time, many years ago in Israel, when another car pulled up alongside me at a stoplight and the driver, young and good-looking, lowered his passenger window and leaned over. "You drive like a man!" he said admiringly.

It was clearly intended as a compliment. What he meant to say was that he thought I drove well. Just as clearly, it was intended as a pick-up line, to be followed by "Let's stop for coffee down the road."

But we never did get to the coffee stage, because the fact is that I have no desire to think or drive "like a man," or "like a woman" either. I want to think and drive like an intelligent person. Yet intelligence on matters of gender is often an elusive quality. To try for it is like entering a heavily marked minefield. Things are likely to blow up in your face at any moment. Maybe it's more of that macho in me that impels me to enter this minefield. Let me be macho, then, about being female.

The truth is that for years I've had an ongoing flirtation with things masculine. That is, with the things men do. I take great pleasure in jewelry and silks and cashmere, but I can also feel great in thermal underwear and desert boots, or a helmet and fireproofed suit. The contrast grabs my imagination, adding to my enjoyment. The undeniable fact of my femininity works with and plays off the socially defined masculinity of garb and occupation. I feel a certain mischievous delight in breaking down stereotypes—in being feminine while acting masculine.

There is defiance in this, clearly. By working in the world of cars, I defy the stereotype of gender. And the attraction of this is not any desire to "become a man." It lies in the experience of a world that was formerly closed to me by virtue of my gender. It is a broadening of my world.

As a child, growing up in heavily sex-stereotyped England, I saw men's lives as more active, more dramatic. Men went out into the world. Women seemed to form their own enclosed worlds. It was quite obvious to me that trains were more interesting than dolls, even though you couldn't sleep with a train. Construction sets were far more fun than dollhouses; a dollhouse came already formed, and all you could do was move the furniture around, but with a construction set, you could make your own. You could *do* things with boys' toys—build, move, crash. You could take over space. A train set could take up a whole room, and a Lego construction could tower or sprawl to limits set only by the number of pieces you had and by your sense of mechanical balance and stress. Boys' toys were a way of expanding into the world, of creating movement and action and presence within it. Girls' toys just were. They came already dressed, already complete. There was nothing to do with them except act out pale imitations of adult expectations.

My brother, three years younger than I, suffered for my cause. I'd drag him out into the woods with me to camp, which he hated. I'd pull him up trees, his fear of falling mirroring my own so that I could be the brave one and he could take on my fear, leaving me fearless. I was acting out my envy of him, of course, for being the privileged one who was not only allowed but expected to do such things. I was not an easy sister.

I took refuge in travel books. I read *The Travels of Marco Polo* so many times that the book fell apart. I read "Boy's Own" adventure stories—my brother's books—and stories of children running away to join the circus, or a fishing fleet, or a cattle ranch. I read about Tibet and South America and the Sahara and Antarctica, anywhere that seemed dramatic and "other."

Even then, unconsciously, I grasped that travel was not a matter of simple geography. It was the mind that traveled. New horizons were a matter of seeing as much as of physical motion. Or rather, of learning to see in new ways.

Early on, then, I saw travel as exploration—not just of a place, but of a culture, a state of mind. It always involved a crossing of boundaries, and conversely, any crossing of boundaries was also a form of travel.

For a woman, entering a 'man's world' is certainly a form of travel, of exploring different realms of interest and intellect. But where we accept boundary crossing in the sense of geographical travel as healthily adventurous, other forms still tend to be less acceptable. Psychoanalysts would say—have said, in fact—that I am refusing to accept my own femininity. In fact, I refuse to accept *their* definition of femininity.

It is simplistic, even crude, to say that a refusal of sexual stereotyping means that I am trying to be male.

When you pit your skills against something larger than you, whether that be the elements or the wilderness or the concrete jungle, you need some degree of physical toughness, to be sure. But far more important is a larger degree of mental toughness—of sheer determination, or what some call grit.

This toughness has nothing to do with swagger. It's a commitment to the task at hand, a willingness to hone your skills, acceptance of a certain level of risk, and above all a desire to do whatever it is well and to enjoy it.

This is a world where you discover your own strength. Men have always been able to do that. Women are only just beginning, participating not as women but as equal questers after that ineffable high of experience, success, and adventure.

Yet even now, at the end of the twentieth century, there is still a bemused suspicion of such women. The phrase "penis envy" rears its head, as though intellectual curiosity and a sense of adventure were nothing more than physiology. What ingrained stereotypes lie behind accusations of trying to be "like men" or "as good as men"? What fear behind what one woman friend said to me: "But you can't really *enjoy* all that. It's really just a way to meet men, isn't it?"

I think it amazing that at this stage in social evolution, anyone should find it surprising that women are driven by many of the same impulses that drive men: human impulses. There is the same basic need to push the limits, to exert ourselves that one step further, to increase our sense of mastery and widen our worlds. And to the extent that this is breaking into a man's world, it is only because physical freedom, discovery, excitement, and adventure have for too long been the domain of men by some implicit unwritten agreement now as outdated as bone stays and hoop skirts.

Exploration, empowerment, drama, challenge, interest, enjoyment—these seem to me essential qualities. They keep a mind curious and thinking. They question the status quo and broaden our idea of what it is to be alive. Without them, life would be closed-minded and narrow. It would, in fact, be unbearably boring.

I suspect this is why macho, in its traditional form, exists. It helps relieve the terrible humdrumness of too many lives—what W. H. Auden called "the ordinary unhappiness of living." It is an attempt on the part of some men to dramatize their lives by exaggeration, to get the blood moving, to rouse passion and action.

But what makes macho so ultimately pathetic is that the real content of life is lacking. Macho is desperate, a cry in the dark, a clinging to the surface traits of socially sterotyped masculinity—to the surface of feeling alive and active in the world.

Cars, of course, can provide this feeling. Especially fast cars, which are a prime source of action and movement. They represent raw power, or the ability to intrude oneself into the world, which classical psychoanalysis tends to take literally as the ability to have an erection, thus reducing complexity to a physical reflex and defining men, insultingly, solely by their genitals.

The fact that cars are sometimes used in this way, however, does not mean that they are, in themselves, no more than an expression of masculinity. We are misled in our thinking about cars by the fact that even now, after a hundred years of automobility, women still give over so much of the involvement in them to men. Although women now buy close to half the cars in the United States, women engineers are a small minority, women mechanics are relatively rare, and there are only a handful of women race drivers. But there exists a multitude of women who love their cars with a passion as great as that of any male teenager and his first clunker. After all, if a fast car can make a man feel more powerful, think how much more it can do for a woman.

Here is a machine that produces power on demand—real, immediate, physical power, tangible in all the senses. You could almost call it a machine specifically designed to enhance women's growing exploration of the possibilities for freedom and control of their own lives.

But every boon bears within it the possibility of bane. Along with freedom and control comes the ability to misuse them. Any highway patrol officer can testify that women now drive as fast and as aggressively as men. And this aggressiveness reveals another, less glamorous, face of speed.

V

SOMETHING HAPPENS TO MY MIND when I drive fast. Speed changes the way I think. The power of the engine becomes confused—or simply fused—with my own personal sense of power. At speed, I feel as though I own the road. Even as though I had conquered it.

This is odd. I have never thought of myself as power-obsessed, or as someone who thinks it important to own or to conquer things or people. I always thought of these as the attributes of tyrants, whether petty everyday tyrants or the kind who control millions of lives.

What speed brings out in me is something far less humane than I like to admit in myself. Something antithetical, in fact, to everything I believe in.

A friend calls what happens to her when she speeds "the maniacal giggle." From her description, it's a more open version of that lopsided grin on my face that I first discovered in the Porsche 911. She drives an old American boat of a car with plenty of good old-fashioned torque, so she can do surprising things on an upgrade. And as she gears down and roars past slower cars, feeling that surge of power beneath her, her eyes light up, the grin appears, and before she quite realizes it, she's laughing out loud.

But laughing at what? I know that impulse myself, but am still not sure exactly what it is.

If I had greater shame, I would not write what I am about to write. I would not want anyone to know. But the daemon is shameless, and although part of me knows I should not write this, I shall do so nevertheless, because it is true. And not just for me.

When you drive fast, you come up very fast behind cars in front of you. If at first this sounds obvious, it has an unpleasant reality on the road. If someone is driving, say, at seventy in the fast lane, and a car doing a hundred and twenty comes up behind, the first driver will suddenly be aware of this shape looming in the rearview mirror that simply wasn't there before. It seems to have come out of nowhere.

Since this has happened to me in the past, I know the feeling. I recognize it in the way the slower driver reacts. There's a double take, a wobble as the driver realizes what is happening, and a sudden lurch to the middle or the inside lane.

This—and here is the real shame—is immensely satisfying to the driver of the faster car.

It seems a gesture of submission. Almost of subservience. As though the slower driver were saying: "Here, I surrender the open space of the fast lane. I bequeath the open road to you, its rightful owner. I forfeit all claim to it."

And then, of course, you are honor-bound to step on the pedal and sail on past, consigning the slower car to the oblivion of the annihilated past.

If you are the faster driver, you don't even need that powerful a car. Nor do you need to honk your horn or flash your lights. You can do it all with relative speed: the rate at which you come up behind the slower driver. "Objects in mirror are closer than they appear," reads the small lettering in the passenger-side mirror of most cars, so if the slower driver is somewhat recalcitrant or unwilling to give way or, more likely, just plain oblivious to what is happening on the road, then you get too close for comfort. You come very close behind, fill the mirrors of the obstructing car, steer left and right slightly to create a wiggle of movement that will make your intent plain, and there you have it: once more the double take, the wobble, the lurch sideways as you sail past with a deep and almost bitter feeling of having finally received your due.

You have exacted the respect you feel you command by virtue of your speed. You have proved your dominance.

It works best with those cars that seem designed to look particularly threatening in a rearview mirror. The Mercedes 500SL, for example, which looks like a steel shark. The Lamborghinis and the Ferraris, with their angular dissonance. Any Porsche, or the Corvette, whose low, sloping hoods look as though they could scoop up the road. These are the fierce cars, the ones that others will defer to almost reflexively. After all, isn't that a major reason for buying them?

The physical danger in driving this way is not because of the speed per se, but because other drivers have no idea of how much faster you are traveling. All they know is that you are going very fast indeed, and this tends to induce panic. You may be predictable. You may even, although this is highly unlikely, be the best driver in the world. But by the fact of your speed, you make others fearful and therefore unpredictable. And in so doing, you make your own road dangerous.

What you are doing, basically, is terrorizing others. And what you experience—if you are honest with yourself—is a kind of übermensch delight. There is an immense feeling of superiority to all else on the road. You are king of the road, master of the universe. No matter that the universe is merely the restricted one created by the tunnel vision of speed, or that it stretches only as far as the eye can see or the memory predict or the radar detector pick up signals over the next hill. Since all else has been annihilated by speed, this world of the road is all that exists. And you are the master of it, the dominator, the one who inspires terror and submission in the hearts of others.

It is a terrific feeling.

It is also, if you stop to think about it, extremely alarming. Let alone petty.

In fact, it is quite pathetic.

In a sense, perhaps all power could be called pathetic. Consider what the power you have at speed consists of. It is mere mechanics: an engine of a certain size, a certain number of cylinders, a spark igniting a mechanism for consuming fuel and for using the energy released by its burning. It is not as though *you* can move faster than anyone else. It is your *machine* that can run faster than anyone else's. The pathetic illusion is the confusion of self with machine.

"I/motor" becomes blended. The machine's power becomes your power. That is one thing, perhaps, with a four-cylinder average family sedan. It is quite another in a twelve-cylinder five-liter, three-hundred-horsepower sports car. That is not the kind of machine that is built for speed limits. It is, in fact, the kind of machine that can be appreciated only way beyond the speed limit. It is a car designed for transgression, one whose very existence assumes that the laws do not apply, thus begging you to consider yourself beyond the law—legal law, social law, and physical law.

This should make you an outlaw. Disturbingly, it does not. If fast cars were banned, then you would indeed be an outlaw. But since they are legal, you are in a strange position—a kind of legally sanctioned illegality.

What you are doing at speed is illegal. You know it, the law knows it, everyone else knows it. Yet you are not despised and condemned for it. On the contrary, when you tell others how fast you were going, you inspire a kind of admiring awe.

Breaking the law is undeniably part of the thrill of speed. Americans who have driven on the autobahn speak of how strange it is to drive so fast legally, with an oddly wistful tone to their voices that says that something is missing. Not only that, they say, but *everybody* drives that fast. And you hear the undertone of complaint. Permission detracts from the thrill. What good is it to be an outlaw in a world full of outlaws?

We romanticize the outlaw, of course. Too many Western movies at too early and impressionable an age. We tend to think of the outlaw not as the hunted but as the hunter. The independent loner. The one who makes his or her own laws and abides by them with an innate sense of rectitude that puts mere legality to shame.

So even though speeding is illegal, it is, for the most part, socially sanctioned. Otherwise law-abiding citizens like myself become lawbreakers at the roar of an engine. And the frisson of delight in this is probably something only an otherwise law-abiding citizen could experience. It is, perhaps, an almost innate resistance to socially imposed restrictions, expressed on the highway because here, enclosed in a car far away from those you know, work with, love, and respect, it is as though society cannot see you.

But breaking the law is only the legalistic side of the real transgression involved, which lies not in the awareness of being illegal but in that übermensch, master-of-the-universe feeling that you are not only beyond the reach of the law but beyond caring about it, as though legality were a mundane encumbrance intended only for those traveling at lower speeds. The world created by speed—that tight, all-absorbing union of driver, machine, and road—leaves no room for social conscience. You feel as though you have stepped into another realm created by speed, and although this realm may seem pure and boundless, it is also very dark. It is, in fact, inherently fascistic.

There are parallels in other worlds of power. There was the socially sanctioned illegality of Wall Street in the 1980s,

fueled by cocaine and greed, in which figures such as Ivan
Boesky and Michael Milken were glamorous—even movie-
role glamorous, as portrayed by Michael Douglas in the film
Wall Street. Political scandals such as Watergate or the Iran-
Contra affair revealed a contempt for law that seemed to
be engendered by power. But the most disturbing parallel
is the rise of National Socialism in Germany in the early
1930s.

The Nazis rose to power legally—democratically. They were
elected, even though their methods, their thuggery, and
much of their outlook were clearly illegal. They made a crass
virtue of the highly romanticized Nietzschean idea of Zara-
thustra flaunting laws, rising above them, and creating his
own. The emphasis on mastery, control, and power glossed
over the illegality in the minds of those who voted for Hitler,
and even made it seem noble.

In this light, that satisfying feeling of superiority with which
I watch others move aside for me on the road is more than
mere rudeness or aggressive driving. It is based on the idea
of those with power dominating an inferior mass. My speed
makes me feel part of a very small, superior in-group, a free
elite of speedsters lording it over law-abiding ants condemned
by their mechanical inferiority to the mundane ordinariness
of speed limits. Who *are* these mere mortals blocking my
way? How dare they?

Others become dehumanized. The blending of "I/motor"
extends to everything else on the road. Other cars become
"him" or "them" in my mind—interestingly, never "her" —
but I do not envision a driver at the wheel. So far as I am
concerned, the car *is* the driver. My dominance is over that

other car, and its driver becomes literally a mere cog in the machine. That machine is inferior, therefore the driver is not even worth thinking about.

Once you start blurring the distinctions between animate and inanimate this way, you depersonalize and dehumanize others. You treat them as though they were objects. There is then no limit to the number of inhuman attitudes that can be attributed to them, and therefore to the amount of inhuman behavior that can be inflicted on them. Every war we have ever seen fought teaches us that. By dehumanizing others, we dehumanize ourselves.

This means that at speed on the highway, I become highly antisocial. Even pathologically so.

However strong the libertarian trend in American culture, the fact is that American roads work because of a strong social contract. Everyone, or at least nearly everyone, obeys the rules. If they did not, the accident rate would be so high that driving would be like playing Russian roulette with five chambers full and only one empty. We do stop at stop signs. We do keep more or less to the speed limit. We do stay in the lanes. We do obey stoplights. In other words, for the sake of both individual and group survival, we submit to a very large body of rules that limit and constrain our behavior on the road. It is probably the strongest social contract in operation in America today, and it works, for the most part, without legal enforcement.

Someone traveling at high speed breaks that social contract.

It has often been said that the road is a place for acting out sociopathic behavior—behavior that is pathological to society—but the truisim hides a deeper and still less palatable truth, as truisms tend to do.

I was a normal, responsible, reasonable driver until I got behind the wheels of fast cars. I still tend to think of myself that way, even when I know that sometimes I am not. A fast car seems to induce a willed blindness in me to the consequences of my own behavior. It seems to call forth another personality, a more atavistic one, capable of a kind of cruelty and ruthlessness that I would never tolerate in the rest of my life, neither in myself nor in others.

Is it mere coincidence, then, that my first experience of this was in a Porsche?

For those with too long a memory, Porsche's history is not quite as respectable as its reputation. The company's founder, Ferdinand Porsche, a brilliant engineeer, had what is in retrospect—and may well have been to him at the time—an uncomfortably close relationship with the leadership of Germany's National Socialists. An obsession with engineering, although it may seem pure and apolitical to those involved in it, is easily manipulated. And Hitler did this perfectly.

In his speeches opening the annual Berlin Motor Show in the 1930s, Hitler continually emphasized the importance of automotive engineering to establishing the might and the status of the Third Reich. Since he himself didn't know how to drive, he clearly had all that more to project onto the idea of speed. Like Olympic runners, race cars became part of the Nazi propaganda effort, and there was no Jesse Owens to blow them away. State-financed German technology dominated the European race circuits as Porsche-designed Auto-

Union Grand Prix cars swept all others aside and set a new world speed record.

At the 1937 Berlin Motor Show, Professor Porsche presented his new "people's car" to the Führer, a car developed at Hitler's behest. At first it was called the KdF-Wagen, KdF being an acronym of the Nazi slogan Kraft durch Freude—Strength through Joy—which soon came to have almost as ghastly a ring as the Arbeit Macht Frei worked into the portals of Auschwitz. The car made it into full production after the war as the Volkswagen.

The idea for the Volkswagen—a people's car—was not original. Hitler got it, in fact, from the United States, and specifically from his reading of Henry Ford, whose antisemitic volume *The International Jew* was on Hitler's desk as early as 1922, along with a photograph of Ford. While the *New York Times* was calling Ford "an industrial fascist" and "the Mussolini of Detroit" because of his despotic style of management, his autobiography was a best-seller in Germany. He is said to have helped bankroll Hitler's Munich beerhall putsch, and in 1938 he accepted the Supreme Order of the German Eagle, the Nazi regime's highest honor for a non-German.

Once war was declared, Ford was pressured into retreating from his openly pro-Nazi stance. But Ferdinand Porsche, like other German carmakers, became even more deeply involved with the Nazi regime. Mechanical engineering was an essential part of the German war effort, and Porsche made his contribution. He designed the Tiger tank, and in 1944 his office was involved in the design of the V-l buzz bombs, self-propelled bombs that terrorized Londoners throughout the blitz. When Enzo Ferrari said that "Porsche don't make racing cars, they make missiles," he spoke a literal truth that he himself wasn't aware of at the time.

After the war, Porsche was interned for two years by the French for his role in the Nazi war machine. On his release, he set up his own manufacturing company together with his son. The first car to carry his name, the Porsche 356, appeared in 1949. Six years later, the twenty-four-year-old James Dean, fresh from playing Jett Rink in *Giant*, would wreck his Porsche 550 Spyder at the junction of Highways 41 and 46 in the California desert, and the Porsche would become the most notorious and desirable of sports cars, absorbing Dean's own legend of glamour and romantic fatalism: sex and death, violence and youth, apparently irresistibly intertwined. The daemon was hard at work again.

Just as the ancient Greeks grasped the inherently antisocial quality of speed in their myths, so too did Hitler, and so, if we are honest with ourselves, does anyone who gets a thrill out of fast driving on the highway. The difference is that we can now do daily on the roads what the Greeks could only dream of. We have the technology to be as gods, and to use it as ruthlessly as gods.

At what stage will we stop confusing ourselves with our technology, mistaking machinery for personal power and glamour? At what stage will we begin to question the purpose, say, of the space effort? Do we really want to colonize space, or use it as a vast arena for war, or, as we seem to be doing most of all, as a vast dumpster for outmoded technology with satellite after satellite pursuing its slow, neverending course through the night sky?

However sophisticated our technology—however well we can tinker with genetics, however many the ways we can split the atom, however fast we can drive or high we can fly—it seems that it will never be enough. Whatever we achieve becomes part of human knowledge, and there is always a further, godlike stage that seems to beckon us, urging us on.

Perhaps the real question is what constitutes sophistication in technology. Is bigger, faster, more, necessarily better? Are there not more subtle ways to use technology? More creative and less destructive ways? Have we, in fact, caught up psychologically with our own abilities? Or are we condemned, for lack of imagination, to curse what our imaginations have brought into being?

VI

THE ODD THING IS THAT MY FIRST CAR was exactly the kind of technology to love, not to curse. It was the "two-horse" Deux Chevaux, alias the Citroën 2CV. And the last thing anyone would expect of a former Deux Chevaux owner is that she suddenly fall prey to the vicious enchantments of speed. After all, the Deux Chevaux was just about the slowest thing on the road. It was the antithesis of the daemon.

Even if it had not been the cheapest car on the market, I would probably still have bought it. You might call it a classic example of imprinting.

It began when I was seven, a restless tourist in the back of my parents' little apple-green Morris Minor together with my brother. Brave parents, these, to put two young children in the back of a car and take off from England to the south of France, especially in 1953, when the English still suffered from that peculiarly provincial frame of mind induced by having an empire, and thought of "the Continent" as unpleasantly exotic. It was odd, daring, even outrageous to so much as think of going there, let alone with two kids in the back seat.

My parents, I now realize, introduced me early to the extraordinary freedom of the automobile. And they sweetened the experience. To ease the journey for all concerned, they placed two large tins alongside my brother and me in the back: one full of barley sugar, and the other full of Fox's Glacier Mints, individually wrapped in waxy blue and white paper with a polar bear printed on it. They assured us that barley sugar and mints would stave off car sickness, and so they did. They also kept us quiet. With one major exception.

My parents' second tactic was to keep us busy, but busy and quiet weren't necessarily the same thing. Count Deux Chevauxs, they said. I can't vouch for how my parents felt about Deux Chevauxs after a three-day drive the length of France (we took it easy, as parents with young children must, stopping overnight in Ham and in Avignon, where yes, we did dance on the bridge, my parents waltzing to a music only they heard). The repetitive chorus of "There's one," the ongoing count, the squabbles over who'd seen more—surely any adult must have hated Deux Chevauxs after those days.

But children love repetition, and the task, together with the candies, kept us happy.

Best of all, there were lots of Deux Chevauxs to be counted. For decades, this vehicle was the cheapest and quirkiest car in the world. In France it was everywhere: the working man's car, the student's car, the housewife's car, the farmer's car. It was the car-about-town, the car that could haul anything. The car that went on working no matter what you did to it. The one car that was an integral part of French life, as no single car has ever been to American life. No mere motorcar, it was a cultural institution—a value system in its own right. France without the Deux Chevaux would have been the States without apple pie.

To anybody English, of course, everything French represents the pinnacle of sexiness, savoir-faire, and joie de vivre. In fact there was nothing sexy about the Deux Chevaux, and the savoir-faire was very down-to-earth, but joie de vivre? That it gave its owners in plenty. Inevitably, years later when I lived in Israel, I would buy one. And it would become my one and only true automobilic love.

It simply never stopped. It could go places other cars dared not. Air-cooled and set high off the road with independent suspension, it was the perfect car for the desert, where it spent the better part of a year as I roamed around the Sinai.

In it, I dodged in and out of battalions of tanks. I drove over a desert track that I was later informed was mined; the car, it turned out, was too light to set off the mines. I took it deep into areas where only Jeeps and camels had gone before.

It was indomitable, and I was indomitable in it. In the French word, *formidable*.

You could do anything in a Deux Chevaux, and that was the whole point. Above all, it represented an idea—an idea of how to live, of how to enjoy having a vehicle that did everything it needed to do, and not one thing more. It was the *vin ordinaire* of French cars, the car for which French roads were built, the car that zipped through every French movie you can remember (and one American movie too: *American Graffiti*).

Clearly, it was not a car for a consumer society, and that too was part of its charm. Its introduction to the States in the late 1960s was a failure, for it was superbly, defiantly, doggedly resistant to everything that sets the testosterone and adrenaline running in the blood of car enthusiasts. It was an environmentalist's car long before Earth Day. A counterculture car long before 1968. A car to induce protectiveness.

I became protective of it because others made fun of it. But if its detractors called it "a tin can on wheels" or "a car designed by a committee," its admirers touted its Art Deco styling and its Bauhaus functionalism. Its technical elegance was pure and simple: elimination. No distributor, radiator, head gaskets. Its character was best defined by the qualities it lacked: power, speed, luxury, prestige, aggressiveness. As the French liked to say, it was to other cars as artichokes are to flowers.

You drove it on momentum. It may have had only a twenty-height-horsepower engine, but those twenty-eight horses could do amazing things on an uphill, provided you took the outside corners wide and clipped the inside ones (already, I was taking racing lines, without even knowing it). If you couldn't exactly win at Le Mans in it, you could, with skill, get up to a reasonable sixty miles an hour, even seventy on a downhill.

You could take out all the seats and have your *déjeuner sur l'herbe* in comfort. You could roll back the canvas top and travel "cabriolet." The air conditioning was simple but effective: a flap below the windshield opened by a lever. And it had real headlamps—not set flush into the body but mounted proudly atop the hood. It also got well over forty miles to the gallon when everything else got barely half that. And since it was so light, if it got stuck in mud or sand you simply got out, provided there were two of you, and lifted it clear.

It was love. True love as only first love can be. Love because of the two cylinders, so reliable that if one went, the car would make it home on the other. Love because it *did* look like a tin can on wheels. Because whatever you did in it, you enjoyed. Because it seemed indestructible. Because it returned your loyalty with its own, never letting you down. (Well, hardly ever.) Because the canvas top rolled all the way back. Because it had a bench front seat. Because the shift stick came out of the dashboard. Because it had flap windows with the lower half locking up into the upper half, so that you could drive with your elbow comfortably aired. Because its windscreen wipers had that comforting tick-tock clockwork sound. Because it could never, ever, go electronic. Because it existed in another world from the idea of a smooth, silent ride. Because even the neighborhood street gang, once they'd scratched their initials into the back, left it alone. Because it had a personality. Because it made me happy.

Which is why the car was in production for forty-three years, and why, when Citroën finally closed down the last plant in 1990, I wrote an op-ed piece in the form of an elegy for it, titled "Adieu, Deux Chevaux." To my delight, the *New York Times* ran it on July 14, Bastille Day. Freedom day.

And now, after test-driving Jaguars and Porsches and Mercs and Lamborghinis, Corvettes and Alfas and Range Rovers, top-of-the-line racy little things and quarter-million-dollar, master-of-the-universe, eight-liter, twelve-cylinder monsters, I found to my amazement that I still missed that two-cylinder, 600-cc piece of tin.

This was not simply nostalgia. I missed the common sense of the Deux Chevaux. I missed the kindness of its technology. In retrospect, even though I could not have admitted it at the time, I suspect I even missed driving slowly.

All this sounds too good. It is. I lie. Not about the Deux Chevaux—everything I have said about it is true, and more—but about its being my first car. There was another car before that, one I prefer to forget. It was faster and more powerful, and it transported me, but it gave me no pleasure and many headaches, and it overheated constantly, so that I became an expert in the ugly art of opening a boiling radiator (a thick rag and lots of patience as you unscrew the radiator cap just a little at a time lest the cap blow and you get a gusher of boiling water in your face).

Aside from standing by the side of the road slowly dealing with the radiator cap, I have no memories of myself in that car. But just mention a Deux Chevaux, and once again I'm driving through the desert in the middle of the night, jackals and wolves in my headlamps, singing Christmas carols at the top of my voice with the windows open and the top down and warm air caressing the back of my neck. That car took me places I never knew I could reach. To my mind, there's no better testimonial to a car than that.

The Deux Chevaux *should* have been my first car. Sometimes I manage to convince myself that it really was. I'm not even sure why I'm now confessing that it wasn't. It has something to do with the daemon again. The daemon is a snob. It can't stand the idea of inhabiting the soul of a former Deux Chevaux owner.

And perhaps it's feeling threatened. After lavishly displaying all its wares to me, it discovers that I still hanker for the sanity of slow simplicity. It suspects that sooner or later, I will turn against the high-performance "ethic" of the internal combustion engine, against the violence it can do to the environment and to our minds.

VII

A<small>T ITS STRONGEST</small>, the daemon is in control no matter what speed I drive. Given no choice, I drive slowly, but it still haunts my thinking.

I certainly had no choice the day a friend asked me about bungee jumping. We were in a Ford F-150, a full-size pickup truck. The size of it made me feel big and bad; in fact, it put me in mind of an old fantasy about getting a tattoo. But no way was this truck going to go fast. So we ambled amiably along the highway, and since we weren't speeding, we talked about speed instead.

Lisa is a bicylist, and compared what I felt when driving fast to the sensation of freewheeling down a steep hill on two wheels at forty miles an hour. The thought of it terrified me and I said so—not the speed per se, but the lack of control on a bike. And that's when she mentioned bungee jumping.

It had just come into vogue: tie an elastic cord round your ankle, tie the other end to the struts of a high bridge, make sure the fully extended cord reaches to just a few feet above the ground or the water, and then jump. Those who had done it called it pure exhilaration.

"Would you do it?" Lisa asked. "Would you jump off a 315-foot cliff on a 300-foot cord?"

I laughed at first. I am not, you see, physically brave. Many people think I am, but much of what I have done—on mountains, in deserts, in various public forums that might best be compared to jungles—has been to conquer my fear, rather than out of lack of it. But as I watched cars speeding past me on the highway, I thought about it further. After all, why not bungee jumping?

What gave me pause, I realized, was that it involved no skill. It seemed to be a matter of pure sensation rather than experience. Yet there were nevertheless certain conditions under which I would be seriously tempted to give it a try.

If my life was full—with work, with love, with interest, as it was at the time, and still is—I knew I wouldn't be tempted. Intrigued, certainly, but no more. I could imagine jumping, but would have no desire to transform imagination into reality. But if I was bored—if there was no work, no love, no project of any kind that could sustain my passion and my interest, as has happened in the past and doubtless will happen again—then quite possibly I'd think "What the hell?"

and do it. Raw sensation would be better than nothing, no matter the risk.

Shortly after this conversation, I came across the psychological literature on risk taking. This work is based on the theory that some people are, by virtue of their metabolisms, "sensation seekers" or "action addicts." As both a former psychologist and presumably a potential subject for study, I was simultaneously intrigued by and extremely suspicious of this theory.

One of the main researchers in the field, Marvin Zuckerman of the University of Delaware, defines sensation seeking as "a trait defined by the need for varied, novel, and complex sensations and experiences and the willingness to take physical and social risks for the sake of such experiences."

That made sense, but Zuckerman then lumped together activities as varied as travel, drug abuse, race driving, and avant-garde art as examples of what he meant. The basic assumption appeared to be that the normal state of affairs is for people to live a safe, secure existence with minimal risk. Those who take on even mildly risky or adventurous activity are then somehow abnormal, and some kind of pathology is presumably involved.

Needless to say, I resented being lumped together with drug abusers as a sensation seeker. In fact, I resented the label altogether. It reduced experience, skill, knowledge, and courage to a matter of mere sensation, which made no sense. If it were simply sensation I wanted, I could down a couple of peyote mushrooms every few days and feel like a quivering mass of sensation while never moving a muscle.

Perhaps to legitimize this labeling, Zuckerman developed a method of measuring his theory— "a sensation-seeking scale" that breaks down into four dimensions: first, thrill and adventure seeking, that is, physical risk taking, as in mountain climbing, race driving, or bungee jumping; second, experience seeking, as in a desire to try new things, whether in avant-garde art or in travel or in drugs; third, disinhibition, meaning the pursuit of pleasure through anything that will loosen inner restraints, such as drinking, drugs, sex, and, oddly, gambling; and fourth, susceptibility to boredom— an aversion to dullness, whether in work or in people.

Both Zuckerman and other researchers claim to have found a high correlation among these four dimensions. This seems odd to me, since it is surely quite reasonable to assume that an aversion to dullness, a desire to travel, and an enjoyment of sex are human behaviors on a very different order from gambling, alcoholism, and drug abuse. But it is amazing what you can correlate with what when you have the right statistical tool at your side and are determined to find some positive correlation. Concentrating on purely physical manifestations helps.

For instance, heart-rate change in reaction to new experiences is apparently higher in sensation seekers than in "others." So is brain-wave response to intense stimulation. Moreover, sensation seekers have relatively low levels of monoamine oxidase, an enzyme that breaks down certain stimulant brain chemicals, whether natural or artificial; as a result, the stimulants last longer and are experienced more intensely (which is why monoamine-oxidase inhibitors were for a long time the antidepressant treatment of choice).

There is even evidence that sensation seekers have higher levels of the sex hormones, testosterone and estrogen.

All this, according to the researchers, means that if you are a mountain climber, a drug addict, or an experimental filmmaker, you are more likely to be sexually promiscuous, to like spicy food, to gamble, and to court physical danger.

Since I am not sexually promiscuous, do not like spicy food, and do not gamble, even though I occasionally do put myself in situations that might be physically dangerous, and since—although I enjoy climbing mountains—I very rarely drink and have not taken illegal drugs since I was a student investigating Aldous Huxley's doors of perception, I began to wonder what world these psychologists were describing. Did it really exist, or did it exist only in their own minds?

The more sensation-seeking research I read, the more I suspected that psychology and statistics were being used to reaffirm preexisting stereotypes on the part of the researchers. With few exceptions, they seemed to have a well-developed sense of the demonic—the clichéd images of sex-crazed drug addicts and semi-suicidal adventurers—but none at all of the daemonic, of that far more complex ancestor of the demonic that included both good and bad, the source of vitality as well as as of potential death.

I began to imagine the researchers as the kind of men who dutifully ran five miles every morning, wore tweed jackets with leather patches on the elbows, sat in "orthopedically sound" armchairs, and tried to figure out why other people were having so much fun. In short, I returned stereotype for stereotype. If I was going to be labeled a sensation seeker, then I would label them armchair psychologists.

It is hardly surprising that the brain chemistry of active people might itself be more active. That does not mean that their activity is explained by chemistry. The question of brain chemistry and behavior is still a chicken-and-the-egg one: which comes first, the experience or the chemical change in the brain?

Neither should it come as any surprise that if we do not use our bodies and our brains, they stultify. Activity diminishes. We do, in fact, become both bored and boring.

Boredom is more than merely a stultifying mood. It seems to be closely linked with depression, and to be the opposite of what we consider the essence of life itself: vitality. In fact, boredom, depression, and death are similar in many ways. All three involve a lack of movement, a stasis or staticness. When life seems dull, we do not feel alive; we feel deadened. So we seek out ways to cut through the boredom and to bring ourselves back to life, as it were. We seek out sensation, in the hope that through sensation, we can arrive at meaning.

Speed obviously can provide that sensation, but it also offers far more. It dares the limits and, in so doing, seems to conquer them. It seems, in fact, to thumb its nose at safety and caution, and to scorn what we usually understand as an innate desire to ensure that we remain alive. Speed reaches for that thin fine line between life and death, that rarefied place where we never feel ourselves so much alive as when we face the possibility of the end of life.

Even as he drives toward death, the teenager speeding home late at night with a couple of six-packs inside him and another on the seat may simply be trying to feel alive. Lacking relevance and meaning, he has settled for stimulation.

The majority of us learn, with time, to live with a certain level of boredom in our lives. Others—and I suspect I am among them—cannot tolerate it. But the ways in which we cannot tolerate it are not necessarily trivial, as implied by terms such as "sensation seeking" and "thrill seeking," or pathological, as in drug abuse and promiscuity. After all, every advance in human knowledge—every scientific discovery or philosophical breakthrough or geographic exploration or creative endeavor—is the result of someone having taken a risk. Someone has rejected the established level of knowledge or achievement, stuck their neck out, and gone further. And people have done this because they had questioning or adventurous minds. Discontent with what already existed, they were unwilling to just "relax and take it easy." And without this combination of curiosity and restlessness, nothing new would ever be attempted, let alone achieved.

Risk taking, in short, is an essential part of human and social vitality. To think of it so literally that you equate it with gambling seems to me to demonstrate an extraordinary impoverishment of the psychological imagination, let alone a peculiarly restricted view of human experience and endeavor. How safe can you play life and still be a sentient, vital, interesting human being? If we were to play safe all the way, we would end up like Howard Hughes, paranoid prisoners of disinfected rooms. We would be alive, but the classic teenager's question is the most relevant comment on this form of life: "What for?"

Sometimes it's enough if others take the risks for us. Not many people have either the skill, the nerve, or the physical and financial resources for the existential high-wire acts of exploration and adventure, so in a sense the mountaineer, the race driver, the test pilot are acting out for the rest of us. The closer their brushes with death, the more we are absolved from brushing against it too closely ourselves. They give us heroics instead of fear and trembling. And therefore we idealize them. Through our heroes of danger, we can live vicariously on the brink.

"Race drivers are not neurotic and they certainly don't have a death wish," says psychologist Keith Johnsgard of San Jose State University, "but they do engage in a hell of a lot of denial." So do we all when it comes to driving, however. Nearly fifty thousand people a year die on American roads, half of them due to the combination of alcohol and driving. That is as many American fatalities per year as in the paddies and jungles of the Far East throughout the whole of the Vietnam War. We know war is dangerous; we deny that driving is. The last thing we think of when we get into a car is the risk of dying on the way to work.

To some extent, denial— "it won't happen to me" —makes life possible. But this does not mean that race drivers are indeed the fearless heroes of popular imagination. On the contrary, they are highly aware of the risks of their profession. How not, when so many fellow racers have been killed or maimed?

Obviously, they employ some degree of denial, but far more important are the practical steps they take to ensure that they minimize the risk, leaving as little as possible to chance. The race is a matter of skill and knowledge and experience— their own, and that of their pit crews and managers. They understand their cars, the dynamics of control, the particular track, their own abilities and those of their competitors, to a degree that raises their driving to a level as different from ours as is a Bach fugue from "Chopsticks."

So far as race drivers are concerned, they are not taking risks so much as exercising their skill. If we think of them as fearless, that is our need. The fact is that a fearless race driver cannot be a good one, but only a liability to himself and others. Some degree of fear—mixed with a large degree of competitive excitement—is essential to maintaining alertness over hours of riding that thin line between life and death, pushing the car to its maximum while judging its limits. In this fine balancing act between nerve and reason, the controlling factor is not risk but calculation. When the margin of error is so small, control is all.

To call race drivers risk takers is so obvious as to explain nothing. To call them sensation seekers is to diminish the art and the science of what they do. It would be closer to the truth to say that they are control freaks—not in the sense of someone who panics when everything is not under control, but of someone who seeks to expand the limits of control.

Paradoxically, what seems to be one of the riskiest of occupations is also one where the highest degree of control is essential to survival, let alone to success. Control is the other side of risk. We are dealing with a Janus here, with two faces of risk, so that to look at one while ignoring the other is inevitably to come to false conclusions.

To some extent, we are all control freaks. In a world where control seems increasingly hard come by—where the fixed rules by which lives were once lived have become fluid, where relationships seem more complex than ever before, where simple communication has become a matter of high technology, where so much is happening that we sometimes feel that we're scrambling just to keep up with our own lives—the car restores a basic feeling of control.

We get in, start up, drive off, and a simple fact of life is reestablished: cause and effect. Gas equals acceleration, steering wheel equals direction. The car responds to what we do, and it does so, usually, without fail. In return for the most basic care—gas, oil, and water—it becomes an extension of the driver's will.

Moreover, the car gives us movement, both physical movement and the sensation of movement in our lives. It enables us to break through the basic feelings of depression: being stuck, in a rut, unable to move. Through physical movement, we reestablish a sense of psychological movement. Behind the wheel, we are back in control.

Control is the essence of the pleasure of driving. But I know I never realized just how essential it was until I put myself in a situation where I could purposely lose control.

I did that by getting behind the wheel of one of Bertil Roos's "slide cars" on the Pocono Raceway in Pennsylvania. Roos, a Swedish champion driver in more categories of race car than most people can name, now runs his own race school at Pocono. He invented the slide car himself, tinkering with the suspension on a regular street car so that above about twenty miles an hour the back end breaks loose, and suddenly you are at the wheel of a car that seems to be in a constant skid. He calls the car "the world's best driving instructor," and he's not a man given to exaggeration.

The slide car is based on the skidpad principle that to learn control, you first have to lose it. When you spin out on a skidpad—a wet concrete circle designed for skidding—you know that you have manufactured that spin by suddenly lifting off the gas and then going down on it again. With some explanation, you can understand why this creates a skid, and that gives you the knowledge and ability to control the spin and stay on course the next time round. But doing all this on the track instead of on the highly controlled area of the skidpad is something else altogether.

The first time I took the slide car round the Pocono track, it was pure hell. I was all over the place. There seemed to be no correlation at all between what I did with the wheel and the way the car moved. It zigzagged all over the place, veered left and right without any warning, and left me feeling helpless and humiliated. It was all I could do to keep it more or less on the track. After two laps of fighting the wheel, I was a sweaty, dismal failure. Beside me, the instructor smiled broadly.

"You look like you're enjoying this," I said accusingly.

"I am," he replied. "So will you."

"Sure," I said, with as much sarcasm as someone who'd just driven so horrendously could muster.

But he was right. A few laps later, I suddenly got it. Keeping my hands fixed on the wheel at a quarter to three helped. So did looking where I wanted to go instead of where I was actually going. Suddenly, instead of battling, I was working with the wheel, constantly steering the other way, driving the track practically sideways with the car in long controlled drifts. My hands seemed to know how to correct for the slide, my eyes to determine where we were going. In a situation that had caused near panic in me a few minutes before, I was now in control. "Good God," I heard myself saying, "this is amazing—I've never had so much fun behind the wheel!"

Afterward, sitting by the side of the track and watching others learn on the slide car, I wasn't even sure which I treasured most, the initial humiliation or the consequent exhilaration. It seems to me that the humiliation of driving without control—the fear and the panic and the experience of it—is an essential memory, literally a vital reminder that control is a matter of understanding and knowledge, that it cannot be taken for granted, and that ultimately it resides in the driver, not in the car.

Speed, then, is not simply a physical thrill. It is a search for an expanded sense of control. But this is one thing on a racetrack, and quite another on a highway. There, when you least expect it, control can be abruptly taken away from you.

VIII

I T HAPPENED ON THE TACONIC PARKWAY going north from New York City, a lovely, winding road landscaped by Robert Moses along the eastern ridge of the Hudson Valley, with two lanes either side and no shoulder. A road built, in short, for pleasure in fast driving.

He was young and he was eager. He was also well hidden in the trees just around a sharp bend. There was no traffic in front of me, so my radar detector remained silent until the very last moment. It blared at the same moment I saw him—a moment too late.

Officer Brennan had blue eyes, a crewcut, and no sense of humor, or at least not one that he was about to display.

He didn't see fit to tell me that this was the first day of a new revenue-boosting drive to issue more speeding tickets in New York State. I'd find that out soon enough. All he said was, "Do you know what speed you were doing?" And then, "Papers, please."

I sat there fuming, watching other cars speed past as he took my license and insurance papers and went back to his car, behind me.

Sooner or later, I thought, as he made his calls and checked to see that I wasn't wanted by the FBI as a dope dealer or mass murderer or income-tax evader, I was going to have to slow down. There was only so long that I could keep on driving at outrageous speeds on the highway without losing my license. This time I'd been lucky; Officer Brennan had clocked me at eighty-four miles an hour. The trouble was, that hadn't even seemed fast to me. Just normal driving. If I'd been consciously driving fast, I'd have been in deep trouble, well over the thirty miles an hour above the speed limit that will automatically place your license in jepoardy. Officer Brennan would clearly have taken great pleasure in confiscating my license.

As I glowered resentfully at the traffic flowing by unimpeded by radar and flashing red lights, it occurred to me that the word *license* was oddly paradoxical. It is used as legal permission and approval—licensed to drive, licensed to practice medicine or law. But it also means freedom, as in sexual license. More than freedom, in fact: a kind of beyond-the-law permission to go wild. So the law gives you license, but withholds it at the same time. Use that license, and you lose your license. . . .

These are the kinds of thoughts you have while you wait for the inevitable ticket and curse yourself for not being quicker on the brakes.

I had, of course, only myself to blame. Since I hadn't been consciously driving fast, I hadn't really been paying attention. Usually, at speed, I was on the alert for radar traps, playing the game of evasion: aiming my radar detector precisely, reading brake lights, scanning the road ahead and behind for telltale signs of flashing lights or cars half-camouflaged in the trees.

The evasion game added to the excitement of speeding, but it also added to the strain of it. It was inevitable that I'd get caught at some point.

Officer Brennan finally handed me my ticket and gave me the ritual warning to heed the speed limit from now on. He waited as I got back onto the road, then trailed me for the first few miles. It is quite disconcerting to drive with a police car on your tail, and I felt very sorry for myself. Legal control had been asserted, and as a result, I had less control on the road. And less freedom. I felt as though my wings had been clipped. Not Icarus falling, but Icarus earthbound.

Reality had caught up with me in the form of unsmiling authority. Transgression is a fine thing until you are caught. Then suddenly the proud defiance melts into a cowed, sullen resentment, made all the greater in this case by the knowledge that I now had a serious problem. With one speeding infraction on my record, I wouldn't be able to talk my way out of a ticket the next time, as I had done in the past. And with four points a ticket, and only eleven points allowable on a New York license, I could lose my license very easily if I kept on driving fast. Lose my license and I'd lose my livelihood.

A speeding ticket could cow the daemon for an hour or two, but that wasn't going to end its hold on me. The car I was driving that day was a mid-range coupe, one of the best-selling cars in the United States; it wasn't considered a fast car, just a regular workhorse. But when I was testing cars made to go a hundred and fifty miles an hour and more, cars that seemed to idle at the speed limit, how on earth was I to keep my license?

The answer, paradoxically, lay in driving fast.

To be more precise, the answer lay in driving too fast—beyond the limits of my control.

Or, to try for still more precision, the beginning of the answer lay in driving too fast. Daemons do not give up so easily.

The twenty-fifth anniversary edition of the Lamborghini Countach, a 420-horsepower, 186-miles-per-hour machine and certainly one of the ugliest cars I have ever laid eyes on, seemed dangerous even at rest on the Chrysler test track in Chelsea, Michigan—two mile-long straights joined by steeply banked U-turns at either end. The outrageous gull-wing design, all sharp angles, made the car look as though at any moment it would take off of its own accord and plow through the small knot of engineers gathered around it, leaving mayhem in its wake.

Jack Stavana introduced himself as "the keeper of the monster." He was in his early thirties, and his good looks were complemented by a well-tailored suit with an expensive flowered silk tie. This was quite fitting; after all, a quarter-million-dollar car demands a sense of style.

I asked Jack to drive the first few laps with me in the passenger seat, explaining that I wanted to get a rough feel for the car and the track before I actually got behind the wheel. How could I say that I was just trying to put off the moment when I'd have to drive it?

He drove three or four laps, and they happened so fast that if I learned anything at all from them, it must have been subconsciously. Since he was also a race driver, he knew how to handle the monster. He didn't tell me that it also helped to have legs of iron and arms of tempered steel. I found that out when my turn came.

It was one of those moments when I wished that I didn't have such a big mouth or such big ideas. Driving the Countach had seemed like a fine thing to do in principle, but now that this principle had become imminent reality, it didn't seem so fine at all. In fact, it seemed downright masochistic. But Jack was already out of the driver's seat and standing by the passenger door, offering his hand to help me clamber out. So I licked my lips—they were peculiarly dry—took a deep breath, and changed places.

I did up the harness and ran through the gears. At least I tried to run through them. It felt more like limping. The clutch pedal was stiffer than any I'd ever come across before, and it seemed like I had to use all my strength just to move the shift lever through the metal gates. "Don't worry," Jack said. "You won't need the top three gears. You'll never get out of third on this track."

"Oh, that's just great," I said pessimistically, shifted into first, let out the clutch, and took off. Almost literally. It was as though I wasn't actually driving. No, I was being propelled, specifically by an astounding three hundred and sixty-nine foot pounds of torque coming from twelve cylinders mounted right behind my ears, midships. The roar of that huge engine reached an earsplitting crescendo as I got up to 9,000 rpm and shifted into second. Never had I had such power behind me. The mile suddenly seemed like a hundred yards, and I'd barely had time to shove the shift into third before the turn was there, crazily sharp, and I had to downshift, using all my strength—my back against the seat to get enough pressure on the clutch, the muscles in my arms straining on the gear lever—and then hang my weight on the wheel as the left windshield pillar came into the center of my line of vision and I found myself staring out the side window at the road ahead. Then down on the gas again as I came out of the turn and into the second straight and the g-force grabbed me, my neck and back straining to keep my head upright and my eyes more or less level, and before I quite knew what was happening, I was halfway up the other straight and had only just gotten back into third gear when the next U-turn loomed right there, waiting for me.

If there'd been time, there would have been a cold sweat on my forehead. If there'd been the luxury of it, I would have been trembling. But at this speed and with this power, time itself was a luxury that didn't exist. It was all I could do to keep the Countach on a good hard line on the track.

I have no idea how many laps I did. I do know that I took it faster on each one. I had to be close to top-ending it, I thought, and then I found the split second to glance at the speedometer: 145. I glanced again and nearly lost control of the car. That was all?

I was mortified. This thing would do 186. That is, maybe Jack could do that speed on this track, but not me. Besides, my desire for the needle to reach that mark seemed to diminish with every lap. This car was too much for me to handle the way it needed to be handled. I knew it, and was humbled by that knowledge.

Finally, I got it up to 155, but by that time my speed was more a matter of pride than of desire. How could I have gotten out of that car and say I'd done less?

"Now take the autocross section," Jack said.

"You're kidding," I replied. If he smiled, I certainly never knew it. There simply wasn't time to check.

I knew I'd never get through it. In a paved part of the infield, the engineers had set up a tight winding course marked with orange plastic cones. The idea was that I would turn off the straight, maneuver through this course, and then get back onto the straight in time to make the next U-turn. In principle, that is. In practice, the cones were dead meat. They scattered like billiard balls as I went veering off course and only just made it back onto the track again. "How do you steer this thing?" I remember asking. It wasn't really a question, and there was no answer.

"Any fool can drive fast in a straight line," Mike Zimicki had said at Lime Rock. I'd just proved him right. And by now I was too scared to be mortified.

When I finally climbed out of that thing, my knees were trembling. I leaned against the car with studied casualness so that nobody could see them trembling. One of the engineers said, "So how was it?" I tried to answer, but no words came. My mouth was too dry.

"I think I need recovery time," I finally managed. To my surprise, nobody laughed. They simply nodded in what looked like sympathetic agreement. I had just found out the hard way that the Countach was notoriously monstrous to handle.

For the first time, the high of speed had evaded me. Somewhere out there, on one of those U-turns, the daemon had faltered, wavered, and lost some of its power. And to my surprise, I was oddly grateful. That was it, I thought. I'd met my match. I'd found my top speed, and any other speed would now seem trivial by comparison.

I felt very mature. I also felt as though something had been lost—some spark of challenge and excitement that had been leading me on. Now I would no longer feel impelled to speed. Or so, at least, I thought I could persuade myself. I was still under the illusion that things were that simple.

I began consciously trying to drive slower. I even started to use cruise control, battling my distaste for it. God knows it is convenient, but I was and still am convinced that it is also dangerous. Put a car on cruise control, remove your foot from the gas pedal, and in an emergency, you will need an extra fraction of a second, maybe up to a full second, to find the pedals again. At sixty miles an hour, say, that's thirty feet of braking space lost. Worse, you may even find the wrong pedal and go down on the gas instead of the brake. In other words, you have lost touch with the car. By using cruise control, you have abdicated control and thus abdicated your responsibility as a driver.

Nevertheless, cruise control could keep me at more or less legal speeds. And sometimes I'd try to convince myself that I *wanted* to be driving at legal speeds. I'd try to remember how it had been in my Deux Chevaux, when sixty miles an hour had been immensely fast, when there'd been time to gaze at the scenery, to look at hawks circling overhead, to enjoy the sky and the landscape. When speed was simply not part of my vocabulary.

Here and there, given a particularly scenic road or an unusually mellow frame of mind, I could still re-create those days. But sooner or later, my foot would creep back onto the gas pedal and I'd override the cruise control. Not up to 155, true, but fast enough to feel the adrenaline flowing again.

It was as though there were some particular dose of speed that I needed, like a fix, to make me feel good and alive and awake. The specific amount changed according to what I was driving and where. It also changed according to my mood or the weather or a whole host of variables that seemed to make my foot heavier or lighter on the gas pedal in never-ending combinations. But one thing stayed more or less constant: once that dose had been achieved, the need for speed was satiated, and I could relax and drive at a more or less legal speed again.

I could get this dose on a track. I still do, fairly often. Like most automotive journalists, I have done several advanced driving and competition track courses, and often manufacturers invite me to test their cars on a track, handing me a helmet and the keys and telling me to have fun.

Occasionally, I even toy with the idea of going into racing. I'm not sure if it is the idea or the reality that attracts me more. I do know that I never knew how competitive I could be until I got into a race situation on the track. Nor how high I could get on taking a sharp corner fast. Or how certain I am that I do not want to die.

Not that I seriously think I could kill myself on a track. Psychologists may call that denial; I call it a certain confidence in my own control. But I do seriously think I could kill someone else—a misjudgment on my part, two wheels touching, the other car flying—and that is quite another matter. I joke to others that I couldn't live with that. But it is no joke.

I have, it seems, a good eye, good reaction times, and plenty of nerve. "Hey, you'd make a good racer," instructors tell me, excited at my zest for speed. And I shake my head: "I don't need to hear this," I warn them. "If I was in my twenties, I'd do it, but your forties is no time to begin racing." And of course they say, "Why not?" and of course I have no answer.

I think that in fact I am simply not ready to invest the time it would take, let alone the money. But I am still flattered that they think it possible, and this possibility tantalizes and persists, sometimes reaching into classic heights of fantasy. When Bertil Roos asked me what was the one article I'd like most of all to write, I heard myself replying, "I'd like to drive in Le Mans, win it, and then write about it."

Each time I get back on the track, any track in any car, the high returns almost instantly. I just want to keep on going, taking it a little faster each lap, a little smoother, a little closer to the edge. . . .The hook is in again. I want more laps, and hate to leave.

Yet when the light dims and I finally do have to leave, the same thing happens each time: I drive slowly. I get back into my own car feeling very mellow and sort of float home calmly, with Mozart or a Beethoven sonata on the cassette player, the windows wide open, and a contented smile on my face.

The pattern is clear: I have been so excited all day, so high from the driving, from the rush of sensation, the stretching of nerves and muscles and alertness, that by late afternoon all I am capable of doing is taking things easy. Back on the road, I am completely relaxed, driving a steady fifty or sixty miles an hour and perfectly content with that, no matter what the car is. It is as though I have driven all the speed out of me. The daemon is sated, at least for the time being, and sits back with a full belly and a contented smile until hunger should rouse it again.

IX

I DON'T KNOW WHY it took me so long to realize that speed is relative. I think that like most of us, I was so focused on that one measure of speed, miles per hour, that I imagined it was an absolute. Speed was speed, I thought. Either you go faster or you go slower. The dial tells all.

But the truth is that the dial tells only a small part of the tale. It gives a physical measure of speed, true, but that may not necessarily have any direct relation to the experience of it. The sensation of speed is independent of the speedometer. Instead, it is a pure manifestation of the Galilean principle of relativity: "All steady motion is relative and cannot be detected without reference to an outside point."

When I drive a race car on a track, I have little visual reference of speed. There is no time to even think about outside points. Since the track is a closed loop, there is little sensation of scenery flying by. I am very low to the ground and the vibration is immense, so that I feel the speed all through my body. But I can't *see* it.

This means that I often feel that I am going far slower on a track than I actually am. The visual indicators I'm used to are missing; I *know* I'm going fast, but my eyes are telling me something else, and the result is an odd disassociation of experience. My mind says one thing, my eyes another. I'm on a racetrack, says my mind; such tracks are made for really fast driving, and at this rev level I must indeed be at high speed. But my eyes say that it doesn't *look* that fast.

Many race fans—and auto racing is now the second largest spectator sport in the United States, after football—might understand this from watching televised races. All such races now include shots taken from cameras mounted on two or three of the race cars. But essentially these shots convey only one element of the driver's experience: the vibration. That, and the noise, tell us that the driver is going fast, but especially on oval tracks where the only scenery is a concrete wall, we have no idea at all as to exactly how fast he is going. Unless viewers have driven that particular track themselves, most would not be able to tell the difference if such shots were taken at sixty miles an hour or at two hundred.

This is most disconcerting, I think, on a steeply banked tri-oval built for continuous speeds of two hundred miles an hour, as is the Talladega Speedway in Alabama. I drove a street car on that track—a Saab 9000—at a steady speed of 140 to 145. That seemed very fast at first, when I was still looking where I would normally look ahead of me on the road. But once I adjusted my vision for the tri-oval, looking much farther ahead—practically to the other side of the track in the turns—the sensation of high speed disappeared altogether. Whenever I glanced at the speedometer, it seemed incredible. The curves were so steeply banked at thirty-three degrees that the car seemed to steer itself around them, with only the slightest pressure on the wheel. My job was merely a matter of keeping steady on the throttle, holding my line, and coming along for the ride. There was no effort. In fact, it was disturbingly close to a Sunday outing.

So here is the ultimate paradox: Speed does not necessarily feel fast. Slower speeds may feel far faster than higher ones. Our perception of speed is not directly related to physical speed. It is flawed. It is relative. It depends on the reference points, internal and external.

This is why it is so exhilarating to drive a little sports car at seventy down a winding country lane—far more so than driving a sophisticated sedan at twice that speed on a straight, empty highway. No wonder Mazda had such success when they introduced the Miata MX-5 convertible in 1989, particularly in a country like the United States where speed is usually associated with size.

Driving the Miata was pure fun. Especially with the top down. It reminded me of the old children's song I grew up with in England: "Boys and girls come out to play. . ." I felt as though I were seventeen again, discovering the delight of motion for the first time. Everything was intensely physical. The landscape seemed to whizz past in a continual blur of external reference points—trees, fences, utility poles, all apparently rushing into oblivion—while at the same time I was aware of the internal reference points of the car itself: the vibration, the noise of the engine, the roar of the wind, all the factors that create the sensation of speed and determine the experience of it. And best of all, although I felt as though as I was going very fast, I was in fact driving relatively slowly, with maximum enjoyment.

By comparison, a high-speed drive in a Bentley Turbo seemed positively staid, even though I cruised in it at 140. The Bentley was a superbly calm and sophisticated machine that cost sixteen times more than the Miata, but it was too smooth, too insulated from all the physical signifiers of speed. The engine merely whispered, and I could have been driving over velvet instead of asphalt. It was built for the self-assured competence of the very wealthy, not for excitement.

For speed to be truly exciting, then, we need the physical proof of it. We need the evidence of our eyes, and we need to sense the raw mechanics in our bodies. The one without the other will not do. We need both.

In fact, physical speed may even be irrelevant. Flying at hundreds of miles an hour in a jetliner can be excruciatingly boring, whereas counter-steering a slide car in a continual drift at thirty miles an hour is pure exhilaration. The difference lies in the degree of active involvement. Speed has to register in our muscles, our eyes, and our brains, creating a generalized physical excitement that we then feel as emotion and exhilaration. We need the sense that we are generating the speed, even creating it, at will. We need, in other words, a certain sense of effort. And we cannot find this without a large element of mechanical rawness.

Our perception of speed, then, and of its correlate, power, depends on physical sensation. The mind needs the signals from the body; the body, the signals from the machine. The more sophisticated the means of speed—the smoother and the quieter—the less our sensation of it will be. The era of the muscle car may be past, but we are still muscle-bound in our attitude toward power. In the age of electronics, we are still addicted to mechanics.

II

IN THE

BELLY OF

THE BEAST

I

SLOWLY, I REALIZED THAT DRIVING is only one way of knowing and experiencing cars. I knew what speed could do to me. And I knew that what I felt was dependent on the visceral qualities of the internal combustion engine. But I still knew very little about how cars worked.

At first, that hadn't mattered. Now it did.

I had fallen into the subject by chance—or so at least I'd persuaded myself—and had a ball driving the cream of the fast-car crop, the full stable of every adolescent boy's fantasies: Porsches, Corvettes, Jaguars, Lamborghinis, open-wheel race cars. I had developed a far greater respect for a good machine than I had ever thought possible. But this respect was still basically one of awed ignorance.

Within a few months, I could use the lingo like a pro. Double-wishbone suspensions, foot pounds of torque, viscous coupling units, limited slip differentials, ABS for antilock brake systems, EFI for electronic fuel injection, HUD for heads-up displays....The vocabulary came easily, even though I had only a vague notion of what I was talking about. I knew what these things were, but not how they worked.

So far as the columns I wrote were concerned, nobody seemed to notice, and this was disturbing enough. But far more disturbing was the fact that I couldn't really appreciate what I was talking about since I didn't understand it. I remained on the level of "Hey, look what this car can do!"

In many respects, that is a perfectly satisfactory level. The whole idea of a good consumer car is that the consumer need not know everything about it to drive and enjoy it. Most cars are designed to soothe the eye and the mind, with all the mechanical details well hidden away. The body is specifically shaped to hide the mechanical facts of life, so that grease can undergo the metamorphosis into fantasy. Even the engine compartment has been cosmeticized. It's not until you compare a race-car engine to a regular one that you realize what effort has been put into making the engine appear unthreatening—compact and smooth and "dressed," with as few naked mechanical parts as possible. And since all cars now are far more reliable than ever before, and most people are content to leave maintenance and repairs to mechanics, the need that a farmer once had to understand his Model-T Ford if it broke down hundreds of miles from the nearest dealer simply no longer applies for most drivers.

Yet I knew I wasn't doing justice to either myself or the cars by adopting such an approach. I wanted to know more. I wanted to know how it was done. I wanted to appreciate the whole thing as far as it could be appreciated. And true appreciation requires knowledge.

I wanted to be familiar with what went on under the hood, to be able to look at an engine and know the car's capabilities from what I saw there. I wanted to break down the barrier of strangeness and incomprehension, and to be on familiar terms with cars—to be able to read them.

But most of all, I wanted to get down to basics. I wanted to get inside the internal combustion engine, as though there, in the belly of the beast, I would find what I was looking for: the structure of the combustion mystique, the innards of my obsession with speed.

And if I was to understand cars this way, from the inside out, then the most sensible way to learn was to become a mechanic's apprentice.

I thought, of course, of the sorcerer's apprentice.

The sorcerer, in my case, was Harvey Penn, who was to be my teacher, my guru, my guide to the mysteries of motors.

Harvey was working at a small, high-quality repair shop called Just Imports in Montpelier, Vermont. Friends in the area had suggested the place, and the owner, Carl von Schummer, seemed to think it quite reasonable when I walked in one morning, introduced myself, and announced that I was good at sweeping floors. Maybe he didn't know how very little I knew. Or couldn't imagine. But he certainly knew how to pick good mechanics.

Harvey was a burly mensch from the Bronx who'd worked on cars for most of his fifty years. He had the bearded face of a rabbi, extraordinary physical strength, and eyes that gleamed with a delight in life worthy of Kerouac at his best. It was just about impossible not to like him on sight, and I was tremendously relieved. I'd been prepared for a taciturn master resentful of a bumbling apprentice getting in his way. But Harvey, I knew instantly, would help me through.

Across the shop from Harvey was Bud Provin, also known as Buffalo Bud due to a close encounter with charging buffaloes on a motorcycle trip out west. Bud was a tall, slim sixth-generation Vermonter in his early thirties with a dry, sardonic wit, a love for country-and-western music, and an ability, as Carl put it, to send any motorcycle out of that shop literally purring. In his left ear, only partially hidden by longish, straight blond hair, he wore a stud BMW earring.

They seemed an unlikely combination at first—different generations, different backgrounds, different specialties, different ways of being in the world—but their mastery of mechanics brought them together in a firm working friendship. Sometimes they sang as they worked, one or the other starting off a whole song cycle that went back and forth for an hour or so at a time. Bud might begin with "Misty," Harvey pick up the theme with "Smoke Gets in Your Eyes," Bud continue it with "Jeepers, Creepers." Or they'd speak to each other operatically across the shop floor, singing friendly insults back and forth.

Neither asked why I wanted to learn mechanics. Only the occasionally curious customer would do that. To Harvey and Bud, it was self-evident. They respected their own expertise, so of course anyone with intelligence would want to know how cars worked. And of course apprenticeship was the best way. After all, that's how they both learned. Harvey at age thirteen in the Bronx, Bud at age eight in his father's repair shop in central Vermont. So far as they were concerned, I was just a late developer.

II

THE MECHANIC'S RAG was the first thing I picked up. Long before I had any right to wear it—if ever I did gain that right—I learned to tuck the corner of it into my pants pocket, letting most of it hang down along my thigh. In some shops they're blue; here they were deep pink, delivered once a month, several gross of them, while the old ones, blackened with oil and grease, were dumped in a big barrel and taken off to be cleaned.

The rag is somewhere to wipe your hands, wipe tools, wipe away grease on whatever it is you're looking at. It's a good sign, this rag. It means that the mechanic cares about cleanliness and neatness. At first, I went sparingly on them.

Then Harvey put me right. "A dirty rag's just going to spread the dirt around," he said. "What do you think they're here for?"

But the rag is more than simply practical. It is a sign of professional identity. Without it, I was just someone wearing a dirty pair of jeans. With it, I was a mechanic, at least in my own eyes.

It worked much like the doctor's white coat, although where the rag has a clear and useful purpose, the doctor's coat defeats its purpose by its very color, and is entirely symbolic. It presents an image of cleanliness and sterility, in the hope, perhaps, that image will become reality. What faith would you have in a doctor whose coat was stained with blood and pus? And how much faith could you muster in a mechanic whose clothes seemed spotless?

After a while, the pink rag became second nature. Or so I liked to think. In the middle of the supermarket, I'd suddenly realize that it was still hanging from my pocket. When I went to pick up parts—an important element of my role as apprentice was gofer—I'd be amazed that the man behind the counter could identify me as coming from Just Imports the moment I walked in the door. Then I'd remember the rag was still there. That is, I'd pretend I'd forgotten.

I admit, I swaggered with that rag hanging out of my pocket. I loved it. I attached so much importance to it, of course, because I completely lacked the real qualities of the profession: the knowledge, the competence, the skill, the experience. Like an actor entering into a part, I latched onto the superficial identifying signs—dirt on my jeans, the rag in my pocket—in the hope that through them I could discover the essence of the role. You might call it the Stanislavski method of mechanics.

So far as the customers were concerned, it worked. I was not entirely surprised. A year or so before, using the journalistic license that allows entry into worlds otherwise closed, I had followed an oncologist friend through a day at his hospital. His nurse gave me a white coat to wear. There was no tag on it identifying me as a doctor or as anything else. But perhaps because of my manner and my English accent, the patients assumed that I was a consulting physician, and deferred to me as they would to one. So too did the nurses on the wards.

I felt uncomfortable. What I saw in the eyes of the patients—hope, awe, even reverence—made me feel like an imposter, a voyeur just looking in on their pain and tragedy, unable to help them. I ended that day with vastly increased respect for my friend's fortitude and determination, but also with a sick feeling inside. I had intended to continue following him, to write an article on him and his work, but I knew now that I couldn't do it. It wasn't because of the sights, the smells, and the sounds of the cancer wards—through writing, I could exorcise those from my dreams—but because of my own impotence and my knowledge that no matter how good my intentions or how willing the patients' cooperation, I would still be intruding on something very private experienced in such a painfully public place as a hospital.

I remembered the look in those patients' eyes when I was working in the repair shop because, oddly, I saw it again in the eyes of those who brought their cars in to be fixed.

Customers who came downstairs from the office—the place was built into a rise above the railroad lines and the river—would sometimes make a beeline for me. Bud would be working hard on a bike and deliberately paying no attention to them. Harvey would be under the hood or the chassis. I was the only one who looked approachable. So approach they did, to ask me how their car was coming along. I'd straighten up, wipe my hands on the rag, and prepare to tell them that Harvey was the person to talk to, but before I could say a word I'd recognize that look in their eyes, and hear in their voices that same reverence, respect, and anxious hope. In their halting trepidation, they might have been asking, "How's my little car doing, doctor?"

In a way, of course, a mechanic *is* a doctor. You go to the doctor when you're ailing, when there seems to be some sort of physical breakdown, and in emergencies, when something is twisted or broken. You take the car to the mechanic when it isn't running properly (a pulled muscle, perhaps, or a limp), when the engine halts or backfires or just sounds wrong (like a congested chest), when it's overheating (running a fever) or just plain broken (a tie-rod end, or maybe a bone).

But mechanics have it over doctors in one important respect: as a mechanic, I could fix something. (Rather, as a mechanic's apprentice, I could help fix something.) It was not a question of take-two-of-these-four-times-a-day-and-let-me-know-what-happens. When we fixed a car, we sent it out of the shop running well. It was an all-or-nothing matter: it worked or it didn't work. If the problem was tuning or adjustment, you could feel the difference instantly. We *knew* when we'd done our job. And so did the customer.

The mechanic wields healing power in a way we only wish doctors did. The doctor's power is a high-wire act; the mechanic's, a logic of cause and effect. Yet like the doctor, the mechanic needs experience and intuition. A mechanic who thinks in terms simply of cause and effect will be good enough, true, but one who has a sense of the life within the engine—what most people know as "a feel" for the car—will be superb.

Harvey had that.

Within two days of working at Just Imports, I knew without a doubt that I had struck lucky. There were few mechanics in the world as good as Harvey Penn.

Exactly how I knew this when I knew so little about cars is something I still don't understand. God knows it wasn't a matter of diplomas or anything like that, for Harvey despised such things. He had gone briefly to a yeshiva after he finished high school, but had dropped out, done his army service, and spent the thirty years since then working on cars, most of that time in other people's repair shops, some of it in the pits at Daytona, and a few years in his own shop not far north of Montpelier, which he'd given up because much as he loved cars, he couldn't say the same for keeping books.

He wasn't tall, but he was broad—a big man with a thirst for life, who threw all of himself into whatever he was doing. Whether that was hard physical work or flopping into an easy chair, the whole of Harvey did it. When I said "Have a good weekend" at the end of the first week, he looked at me in astonishment. "But of course!" he said.

To my delight, he was a natural teacher who worked out loud, talking about what he was doing as he was doing it. We quickly developed a kind of doctor-nurse routine, with me watching over his right shoulder and handing him the tools as he worked, until soon he decided I'd watched enough, simply handed me the power wrench or the oxyacetylene torch, and said, "Here, you do it." And to my amazement, I did.

All those years working on cars had left their mark on him. Many marks, in fact. It took a few weeks for me to compile just a shortlist of his injuries. "There've been so many," he said wonderingly when I asked him. "I've lost track."

There was the road accident when he was nineteen, which had him in and out of the hospital for well on a year, with multiple operations on his leg and hip. That left his left leg so deeply scarred that the scars were like furrows in the muscles of his legs, twisting them out of place. Add to these more scars caused—scar tissue over scar tissue—when he was trapped in a pit fire a couple of years later, down beneath the car when the oil began to blaze, and the only way out through the flames. Then there was the motorcycle accident; that got his collarbone. And in 1980 he'd been diagnosed as having multiple sclerosis, which meant that sometimes his muscles, already cramped in their twisted paths over his leg bones, would cramp still further. He took painkillers for the cramps, but being an all-or-nothing person, he took too much at one time and then was left short on other days. They were the bad days.

It didn't seem to occur to Harvey that there was anything unusual in this mass of injuries. If you were going to hang around cars, you'd realize soon enough that flesh was weaker than metal. Until I actually saw him shoulder a transmission case and carry it out to the yard, it seemed impossible that anyone so injured could have that much physical strength—or that it could be combined with such gentleness. It was a beguiling mix.

When his wife, Gladys, a social worker, came home with stories of domestic violence toward women and children, he was shocked. He simply could not understand it. And when a raccoon began to haunt his trash bins, he went to extraordinary lengths to scare it off, staying up at night to drop water-filled plastic bottles near it. When I remarked that by altering his aim slightly he could simply kill it, he recoiled. "Why would you want to kill a raccoon? They're beautiful creatures," he said, and went into a near rhapsodic description of the handlike paws and the face, "like a little human with goggles on."

Free now of his own shop, he spent half of each year in Vermont and half in Florida, working as an itinerant mechanic on an hourly wage. It seemed a poor arrangement for a man known locally as "the king of torque," who could tighten a bolt so precisely by hand that if you checked it afterward with a torque wrench, you could only stand back in amazement at the perfect reading. But he had his freedom, and he had his own land on which to enjoy it.

He'd built a magnificently quirky four-storey log cabin into a hillside with some forty acres of land around it, where he waged a running battle of wits and willpower with beavers, raccoons, and deer. The front yard was full of cars, each in one stage or another of care and attention. At any one time, the majority ran perfectly, and every spring and fall Harvey and Gladys would run several of them up or down the East Coast in all-night runs, making the return trip by train. They were nearly all big solid American cars, the prize being a perfectly maintained 1965 pale yellow Cadillac. The one exception was Gladys's little Mazda 626, a car Harvey referred to, as he did all small Japanese cars, as "the heliotrope." I'm not sure he knew exactly what a heliotrope was—I had to look it up in the dictionary myself—but it didn't matter. Somehow, in Harvey's mouth, the word was perfect, calling to mind the putter of helicopter rotors together with something so light it floats up toward the sun.

I didn't know all of this at first, of course. I simply trusted Harvey almost on sight, as did those customers who made their way down to the shop floor. There was something about the way he behaved around cars, the way he worked on them, that left you with absolutely no doubt that he understood them perfectly. He didn't love cars with that investment and projection of ego you find in so many car owners. He cared for them, and that care came from a depth of understanding that precluded romanticism.

He had, above all, a sense of the harmony in a smooth-running motor, one that was satisfied every time he sent a car out working well, and that was deeply offended every time a car came in that had been neglected.

I never met the owner of the red 1976 Porsche 924. Harvey and Bud assured me that I didn't want to meet him.

The car was a mess. The owner had finally brought it in because the rear brakes had gone, the handbrake had gone, and the front brakes were about to go. The front brakes had apparently decided him. Not to mention the fact that most of the underside was in advanced rust from the salted winter roads of northern Vermont, that the air-conditioning radiator looked like someone had been hammering on it, that the engine was incredibly filthy and many parts rusted, and that it was unclear if the other half of an old half-eaten bagel in the back seat had been eaten by the owner or by mice. More, the owner had tried to weld a loose hinge in the driver's door and in so doing had managed to burn the hinge and jam the door completely. Oh yes, and he'd said he'd also been having difficulties getting it started.

Perhaps inevitably, I thought of the Stephen King novel *Christine*, which was made into Steven Spielberg's first movie. In this tale of demonic possession, Christine is a 1957 Plymouth Fury with a diabolical personality. The young man who buys the car as a near wreck and fixes it up becomes first obsessed and then possessed by it, until the car, after killing off various other people, kills him off too.

Like Christine, the red Porsche seemed to emanate what would once have been called bad vibes. It was almost as though it glowered at us in sheer resentment of its abuse. It was there, in the yard, from the first day I arrived at Just Imports. It would still be there when I left. The owner was in no hurry to get it back, and this surprised nobody. We worked on it when we had nothing else to do.

"*You* climb into that thing," Harvey said in disgust, and I squirmed in through the passenger door, over into the driver's seat, and started it up. The car made a peculiar sound as I backed it up to the hydraulic lift, creaking and grating like a haunted house. The shocks were almost gone. I got it into place and automatically went down on the brake. Nothing happened. "Pump the brakes quick!" shouted Harvey, and as I did so, he put all his weight on the front end, pushing against the car's momentum.

Finally, we got it up in the air, took off the wheels and brake covers, and found no linings at all left on the rear brake pads. The discs in front were barely passable. There were several oil leaks.

I'd never seen an expression of such distaste on Harvey's face, not even face to face with the tinniest of heliotropes. "This car is an insult," he declared. It was the antithesis of everything he appreciated in mechanics: harmony, smoothness, cleanness. The Porsche's owner had taken a superb machine and, through sheer neglect and what seemed utter lack of feeling, turned it into something that should not have been allowed on the street. Into junk.

What did this owner feel, I wondered, driving a car with next to no brakes? What was he working out on the road? Did it excite him? Was he a man so controlled, so aware always of exactly what lay around the next corner in his life, that the car was an escape, a reaction against all that? Or was it more direct: the car as an expression of his own headlong blind lurching into the unknown? Into self-destruction?

I knew it had to be one or the other, but Harvey and Bud were right: I really didn't want to know which.

III

HARVEY CARED VERY DEEPLY about cars, but he was not obsessed with them. Not for him the blurring of "I/motor." He understood cars as machines, not as extensions of his own self.

Most of us are not so lucky. We identify strongly with our cars. We have a lot invested in them: our sense of self, our sense of freedom, and for many, like me, our sense of being adult, of being in control of our lives. We depend on the car to move, to get to work and back, to go visit lovers, or just to get away. We use cars to impress others with our taste or our status. In short, there are such a host of reasons for attaching so much importance to an engine, a steel body, and four wheels that when our cars break down, so, in a very real sense, do we.

"Automotive deprivation syndrome," an architect friend used to call it. He was only partly joking. When his car was in for repairs—as it often was, for he drove it hard, didn't care for it well, and seemed to imagine that it would last forever, as he did his own self—he reacted badly. At best, he would mope. At worst, he'd be restless, fidget, yell, even throw temper tantrums. He couldn't work, couldn't concentrate on anything except the one overriding fact that he was deprived of his car.

His car was broken, and so was he. He was like an actor without a voice, a writer without a pen, a mechanic without tools. He was lost. Frustrated. Isolated. Angry. And hurt.

It was as though he were being forced back into adolescence. Into the time before he ever owned a car.

His was, admittedly, an extreme case. But to some degree we all go through it. I had one car that was very close to being a lemon, so I know of this. I took it very personally every time it broke down. If the tires were out of alignment, so was my life. If it was having transmission problems, they were there in my life too. When the tires wore down, I'd feel worn down. When there were timing problems, I felt out of sync with the world.

The car was like the innards of the slaughtered goat: in its manifestations, I read my own. Its breakdowns paralleled mine. And when the car was due for its road test, I'd feel my adrenaline rising and my palms become damp as though I myself were to undergo the test. When it passed, newly licensed and ready to go, I felt high, as though I myself had passed *summa cum laude*.

Not being a mechanic, I completely lost sight of the car as machinery. In short, the car became me—free and powerful when working well, and miserable for myself and others when not.

One of those times was in the Citroën Deux Chevaux. It was the only time it failed me, but it was, to put it mildly, inopportune: halfway down a very steep and very rough mountain track in the middle of the Sinai desert. Two friends were with me at the time. They told me later that when I said in a very quiet voice, "We've got no brakes," my face went visibly white under the deep tan. I didn't notice what color their faces went.

We got down the mountain on the gears, and when we finally reached a small town and found a mechanic, discovered how simple the problem was: a kink in the plastic tubing of the brake-fluid line, formed during all the bouncing over boulders up in the mountains. It was the kind of problem that I could spot by myself now, but at the time I didn't even know where to start looking. One of my friends took a photo of me just after the brake line had been straightened out. I never thought it was possible to smile literally from ear to ear, or that plain relief could look so good.

I thought of that day many years later when my right knee went as I was scrambling down a steep slope in the Sierras. I got down that one too, with great pain, and discovered that knees don't heal as fast or as well as brake lines. But the parallel was there: knees, brakes—all a matter of control and of freedom to wander.

The knee problem continued. Chondromylacia, said the doctors, but all I knew was that although I could continue hiking and climbing, if with greater care than before, my running days were over. And now that I think of it, there may well be a connection between the fact that my knees had gone and the beginning of my involvement, a couple of years later, with cars. I know I felt horribly grounded once I realized that I couldn't run anymore. And I know too that in a fast car, I can outrun the wind. If I told others as a matter of convenience that my involvement with cars began as a result of pure chance, the truth is that such chances are caused by something. As an old and wise friend once said, "Luck happens to those who are ready for it." My knees were weak, ergo, I was ready for cars. They could give me back my mobility.

You would think that the symbolism of cars and their relation to human bodies would be a matter of fascination to psychoanalysts. They could have a field day. Yet, although I've searched through a vast mass of psychoanalytic literature, I've found practically nothing about cars. It is as though analysands never drive. In fact, maybe they don't; many analysts and their patients live in Manhattan, which is a driver's nightmare. But more likely, this peculiar absence of so potent a totemic symbol is a sign of a certain intellectual disdain for things mechanical.

Automakers have certainly not been nearly as prudish as psychoanalysts. In fact, they have gone to extraordinary lengths to create an image of cars as something more than complex pieces of machinery. Outrageously sexist car ads—

selling cars, like beer, by implying that the right one will bring a man a bevy of lubricious young women in various states of undress—are still a stock tactic for some companies, who seem to be blithely unaware that only a little over half their customers are male. We may be past the time when a car could be advertised with a young woman in a bathing suit posing as a hood ornament, but automakers haven't come a long way at all, baby or no. Shift sticks of fast cars are still ridiculously phallic; some auto designers still talk of the car itself as a phallic design, which certainly says strange things about their own body image; and certain television commercials still play on extreme phallic images of thrusting oneself into space.

Then, of course, there are the names. They may be fast "macho" animals, like jaguars, mustangs, bearcats, and broncos, or masculine icons such as rangers, chieftains, and troopers. Or with the fastest and most expensive cars, they may go for obvious sexual wordplay, such as the Countach and the Testarossa. All these names invite projection, an obvious acting out of other, fantasy lives. They invite the blurring of "I/motor."

Detroit is still the leader in this image-making game, with the Italians tagging along behind. The Germans are the most reserved, naming their cars by numbers. The Japanese play it safe either with numbers or with sexually neutral names. Since both German and Japanese cars have a reputation for high quality, it seems time for Detroit to consider the possibility that mechanical quality and sex may not be a very good mix.

Still, I can understand why that mix is so tempting. Consider the everyday terms in the world of engines: push rods, ball bearings, pumps, power strokes, drive shafts, vibration, lubrication, AC/DC, bodies, couplings, friction, heat. . . . Inevitable, no matter your gender, that here and there the double entendre raises its head.

And in the repair shop, it did. Regularly.

We'd get into these sexual puns for a few minutes here, a few there, maybe once or twice a day, and then as we concentrated on the job at hand, we'd lose consciousness of them again. They ran in little riffs, with a burst of awareness, and then suddenly there was nothing you could say that did not have a second meaning. But they then became so obvious that they didn't keep our attention. Real attention was always focused on the work at hand. The rest was a sort of trilling of other parts of the mind, which is why things were so relaxed and easy—why, no matter how raunchy, the double entendres were never serious or insulting.

I still don't know if they were there because I was. A woman in what is usually an all-male setting inevitably raises an awareness that isn't usually there. Working with that language day in, day out, over decades, Harvey and Bud had surely lost awareness of its sexual possibilities; my presence reminded them. As did the fact that the language was new to me, that it struck me more than it did them, so that sometimes the ripple of double entendres would start with me—with a pause, a look, a grin, and then a riposte. It was a mild form of flirtation, perhaps, an assertion of my own femininity in this masculine environment. Or simply an enjoyment of language. Or all these things together. Whichever, it was fun.

Besides, sex was only part of the analogy between car and human. The engine could easily be seen as a heart, with the pistons pumping away inside the cylinders and the valves opening and closing. Or the wheels as feet, marking up the miles. Or steering as control—steering your life. The drive shaft is surely the spine; the suspension arms could be human arms; the joints, human joints. Braking, accelerating, speeding, overtaking, being stuck in a traffic jam—you don't need years of psychoanalytic training to grasp the symbolism inherent in these actions. The car becomes us; we become the car. Christine lives.

IV

WITH BUD AND HARVEY'S HELP, I eased into the daily routine of the repair shop fairly quickly. My Vermont friends were both curious and supportive. After hearing me talk about the shop, they began bringing in their cars to be fixed. Their attitude was in sharp contrast to that of friends and acquaintances in Manhattan, among whom my decision to seek out an apprenticeship had aroused a surprising amount of opposition.

Some had laughed and said, "Oh, you're just being macho again." Others teased me about being a grease monkey, or simply made it clear that they thought I was taking this new-found interest in cars one step too far. The most outspoken view was also the simplest: "Are you crazy?" said one close friend. "What on earth would you want to do that for?"

So long as I was driving fancy cars—status symbols—that was passable, even amusing. But to get grease on my hands was something else altogether. It made people oddly uneasy.

This still puzzles me. I am talking about highly intelligent people, all of whom drive cars. They need cars in their everyday lives, or at least for the weekend getaways that they consider essential to surviving life on such a stress-filled island. They are, in other words, dependent on cars, as we all are. Auto dependent, some call it, clearly relishing the connection with alcohol or drug dependency. But of any group in society, it is perhaps intellectuals who understand the least about cars. And perhaps out of resentment over this, they tend to ignore them as a fit subject for inquiry.

Not that I had been at all different. I had, after all, spent the better part of my first year as an auto columnist in a state of somewhat embarrassed confusion. But eventually I realized that this embarrassment was double-sided. On the one hand, an interest in cars apparently indicated a certain superficiality of mind. On the other, my own vagueness as to exactly what happened under the hood made me feel superficial. But to make myself less superficial in my own eyes was to make myself more so in the eyes of others. Appreciation of cars is generally relegated to "car buffs," and "buff," as in "Civil War buff," implies an impassioned amateurishness, as though the interest focuses for the most part on surface details, on the intellectual level of "Jeopardy" or "Trivial Pursuit."

Nevertheless, an intellectual interest in the Civil War is perfectly respectable, and hundreds if not thousands of academics are making their living precisely this way. But an intellectual interest in cars? That sounds like an oxymoron. Cars are understood to be part of what is known as "popular culture," and aside from a few forays into the field by French philosophers such as Roland Barthes and Jean Baudrillard, they are generally considered unworthy of serious intellectual pursuit.

The only truly acceptable intellectual nod to popular culture in America comes with baseball; nearly every red-blooded American writer has written something about the game. But cars have been left to the rebels. The beat poets, and especially Kerouac in the famed *On the Road*, celebrated the car as freedom and escape. Harry Crews explored the way we project and incorporate cars into our lives in his novel *Car*, about a man who eats one, bit by bit—a tad too outrageous, as Crews tends to be, for literary acceptability. And science-fiction writer J. G. Ballard took the link of Eros and Thanatos literally in his quasi-pornographic novel *Crash*, whose protagonist gets sexually excited by crashing into other people's cars; in a new sexuality born of a perverse technology, he drools over the idea of "the whole world dying in a simultaneous automobile disaster, millions of vehicles hurled together in a terminal congress of spurting loins and engine coolant."

On the more mundane side of things, there is a plethora of copiously illustrated books on "the role of cars in American life" or "the automobile and American society," cultural-historical surveys purporting to explore the cliché of "the American love affair with the car," as though nobody else loved cars and as though a love affair—any love affair—could be explained by simply calling it that.

The exceptions, of course, are Lewis Mumford and Ivan Illich, both of whom wrote with particular prescience about the way cars were changing American life. As early as 1956, Mumford was advocating the use of electric fuel cells, instead of gasoline, to power cars. Yet even as I read them and agreed with them, deploring the destruction of cities, the fractionalization of social life, the paradoxically increasing isolation made possible by the very machine that should have made it easier to be with others (in much the same way as the telephone has increased isolation instead of decreasing it)—even here I got little sense of the real power of cars over our imaginations. Anyone trying to explore that mystique is in danger, as I no doubt am, of being relegated to the status of car buff, grease monkey, girl racer, motorhead.

Such an attitude has rationalizations galore. It is easy to despise cars for the way they are marketed, the rate at which they kill when driven badly, the way they act as an outlet for the grosser aspects of macho and adolescent bravado, and especially the way they pollute the environment. It is just as easy to ignore the way we are mystified by them, and therefore resent them precisely because we are dependent on them.

This is a dangerous blindness. Unless we can understand the power that cars and driving have over our lives—what keeps us dependent, what pulls us to cars, what excites us about them—any critique of them remains on the purely intellectual level, divorced from the reality of our lives and our roads. The more unaware we are of how cars affect us, the less we will be able to confront and control the damage they do to our minds, and to our planet.

Still, there was something underlying the opposition of my Manhattan friends that seemed to go further than simple resentment of dependence on cars. I couldn't quite put my finger on it until one day I was talking to a homeless man who lived in my neighborhood. His story was that he had been a jazz musician, picking up a gig here and there and taking too many drinks and too many drugs. Then someone stole his saxophone, and now he was living in the park year-round. "Just taking a break for a year or two," he said by way of rationalization.

We were sitting on a bench in the sunshine, drinking coffee, when he asked how I'd be spending the summer and I told him I'd be working as a mechanic's apprentice. He got very upset, even agitated. He leaped up from the bench and began pacing as he lectured me: "What do you want to do that for? That's manual labor! Why does someone like you want to do that? That's going down, and you should be going up, not down."

He meant down in the sense of class, I realized. Socioeconomic class. This man, at the bottom of the class pile, was deeply upset that someone like myself, in the upper-middle range of the pile, should want to do anything that would lower my place in it.

I sat there listening to him, the coffee going cold in my hand, dumbstruck by the ironic counterpoint of the situation. Until then, the issue of class hadn't occurred to me. I needed a homeless jazz player to point it out to me.

Not only had I committed cultural transgression by my interest in cars. I was now about to commit class transgression too by going to work on them.

I knew, of course, that cars are class indicators, and particularly powerful ones because of their visibility. By then I could practically tell someone's income by the car they drove. Yet class is far more than just money. Even the most beat-up old jalopy, if driven with a certain panache, can be a status item. Only a shabby mid-range or small car that has been uncared for and used merely as a utilitarian runabout lacks class—but even then is not lower class. There is, in fact, no such thing as a lower-class car anymore, especially not since the pickup truck has been adopted by the sun-and-surf set.

Yet the mechanic who cares for a high-class item such as a Porsche or a Jaguar is what the English used to call lower class: a working-class man. A man who does manual labor.

This much I realized before I began working as an apprentice. But what I could not grasp until I saw it is that the moment something goes wrong with the car, the whole balance of power changes. For the exact span of time that a car has problems, the owner sees the mechanic as possessed of some mythic power. All consideration of class disappears. Or at least, the owner tries to make it disappear.

It was a BMW 535, just a few years old, but salted winter roads had taken their toll, especially on the exhaust. The owner, a doctor, had driven it a hundred miles to get it fixed at Just Imports. That's how good the shop's reputation was. It was going to be a big job—we had to replace half the exhaust system—and because the owner had come so far, we'd have to get the whole job started and finished the same day. He'd wait.

The doctor had never been to Montpelier before, but despite its picturesque appeal, he wasn't interested in looking around. The farthest he strayed was across the road to pick up coffee and a bagel and then he was back, perched on an empty motorcycle table in the middle of the shop, drinking in the atmosphere, the smells, the repartee, along with his coffee.

He clearly adored Harvey, who was in fine form that day, full of stories of Vermont in the 1960s, with wild days and wilder nights. But he wisely kept his distance from Bud, who was in one of his cool, don't-touch-the-master-of-the-art moods.

Watching him as he watched us, it seemed to me that he was fascinated by what he thought of as the proletarian romance of the repair shop. Sometimes he seemed like a boy excited to be in the presence of masters of the art of making machines go—magicians of motion.

He spent most of the morning with one leg perched up on the motorcycle table, the other dangling to the floor. To judge from the creases of strain on his pants, it must have been a very uncomfortable pose. Soon he was telling jokes—off-color jokes, which were as out of place here as he himself was. Bud and Harvey smiled and laughed appropriately. Harvey winked at me and shrugged. I managed a wry grin. But the grin disappeared when the sex jokes gave way to a worse kind of talk: the doctor began to tell us how little he earned.

He was driving an expensive car, true, but he went to great lengths to explain that he had bought the lease from somebody else as part of a new job, which was good because of course he couldn't possibly dream of buying a new BMW outright, they cost so much, they're marvelous cars but terribly overpriced, and so on and so on. After all, he said, he probably earned less than Harvey and Bud.

I just stood there, wrench hanging by my side, and stared in amazement. Harvey and Bud handled it better. They were used to it.

"Yeah?" said Harvey. "Well, you heard about the plumber who does work in a doctor's house? The doctor complains about how much it costs and the plumber says 'I know what you mean, I used to be a doctor myself but I couldn't afford it anymore.'"

And without missing a beat, Bud added, "Yes, and when he became a plumber he learned how to lie."

In fairness, the doctor may have been feeling somewhat guilty. After all, here were these superb mechanics working their butts off for a mere ten dollars an hour. Or perhaps he thought they received the whole of the shop rate, which that summer was thirty-five dollars an hour, although even that can only have been a fraction of his hourly rate. But more important, it was as though, for the space of time that his car was in their hands, he felt a compulsive need to establish himself as one of them.

"You don't find it insulting?" I asked Bud after Harvey and I had gotten the exhaust fixed and sent doctor and car back home.

He shrugged. "Happens all the time. Maybe they think they're going to get ripped off if we think they're too wealthy."

"What about all this dirty joke business?" I said.

Bud gave a soft sigh of resignation. "Just trying to be one of the boys," he said.

"What does he think he's doing?" I asked. "Slumming?"

Bud nodded. "Something like that."

Harvey just stood there admiring the twenty-dollar bill the doctor had given him as a tip. "Class act," he said wryly.

A broken car reverses the usual class order. For as long as it is out of order, the owner is stripped of a major symbol of his or her class. The problem seems to be worse for men than for women, perhaps because women tend to invest less of themselves in their cars, or because they are more ready to acknowledge that they can't handle the problem themselves. In the depths of automotive deprivation syndrome, many men clearly feel less sure of their class, their status, their power, even their manhood. And the mechanic has it in his power (and sometimes her power, thus further complicating the issue) to restore all this.

The doctor told dirty jokes not just because he was trying to be one of the boys, or to ingratiate himself, or to participate in his idea of the romance of the proletariat, but also because he needed to reassert his manhood in a position of powerlessness. Perhaps, in fact, that is always why people tell dirty jokes.

With that gracious tip, however, the whole deal was off. Power had been restored to the doctor, and he could reassert his class. The moment the mechanic fulfills his role, he loses his aura, his mystique, his magical powers, and becomes once again a working-class man to be paid off and forgotten—until the next time.

V

"**O**H GODDAMN," BUD SAID. Almost quietly, as though to himself. I had my back turned to him at that moment. He said it as though he'd forgotten something, left some essential tool at home.

But Bud never swore. That's why I turned round. That's why Harvey looked up. That's how we saw Bud leaping around the work table to try and catch the bike as it fell away from him.

He didn't make it.

"It happens," Harvey kept saying after the three of us had righted the bike. Bud was pacing like a caged animal. "Not to me," he said between clenched teeth. The fact that he'd nearly been crushed, or that the bike could have been badly damaged, was not what was eating at him; it was the reflection on his professionalism that hurt.

"Good mechanics are egomaniacs," he'd said to me once, as we were working together on a transmission case. I'd been re-reading Robert Pirsig's *Zen and the Art of Motorcycle Maintenance*, and I'd asked Bud what he thought of it. When it first came out, in 1974, I'd skipped the parts on motorcycles and read the rest. Now I found I was skipping the rest and reading the parts on motorcycles.

Bud turned out to be a tough critic. "First, there were mistakes in the stuff about motorcycles," he said. "Second, that's a weird book: 'I was once a brilliant man but then they electro-shocked that man out of me and now I'm someone else.' But that guy had one really good point: good mechanics like to be right. And there's always a competitiveness going between them. It's friendly, but it's serious too—who can diagnose a problem best, who can get it right. They take pride in doing things properly."

"You must be talking about the kind of mechanics car owners never meet," I said.

"No, I don't think so. I think most mechanics are like that."

"Most good mechanics, maybe," I said. Bud shrugged and tried to hide the smile of pride.

The bike he was working on at the time had crashed, and he was drilling out a smashed bolt and rethreading the hole, with such absolute precision that Harvey came over and just stood and watched in admiration. "That thing's going to be better than it was before the crash," he said.

"We're just doing it properly the way they didn't do it at the factory when it was made," Bud replied.

That was certainly the statement of an egomaniac. He said it with a carefully nurtured insouciance, but he was absolutely serious too. And after working alongside Bud for a while, I began to think maybe he was right. About the quality as well as about the egomania.

Mechanics run in Bud's family. He started working in his father's Triumph motorcycle shop in central Vermont when he was eight. His great-grandfather had been the first mechanic in the family, and one day—a good day, with the work flowing well and the mood relaxed and bluegrass music playing softly on the small cassette deck hung on a hook over the sliding doors—Bud told the story of how the old man once nearly cut right through his finger: flesh, tendons, and bone. It was smashed, but not severed. He took one look and realized that the finger was lost, so he wrapped it in a cloth, called over his assistant, gave him a heavy brass hammer, laid a knife over the wrapped-up finger and said "Hit the knife." When he uncovered his hand, the assistant fainted. The old man threw away the finger, drove twenty miles to the nearest doctor, had the stump cauterized, and was back at work the next day.

It was a perfect Vermont story, worthy of *Yankee* magazine. And Bud was pure Vermont, with a Vermonter's disdain for "flatlanders" from anywhere south of the Green Mountains. When Harvey said someone had told him that since he'd been around Vermont for over twenty years, he could stop considering himself a flatlander, Bud's response was so quick and sharp his great-grandfather would have swelled with pride: "Oh yes, and how much money does he owe you?"

Then he told the story of a young New York couple who'd moved to Vermont, had a child there, and fondly imagined that their child was a native Vermonter until his great-grandfather had said, "I see, and if your cat gave birth in the oven, would you call those kittens biscuits?"

The banter between Bud and Harvey was often funny, sometimes sharp and competitive, the kind of banter that might give offense elsewhere, but that here was held in check by their respect for each other's skill as mechanics.

"It's a small world," Bud might say, talking about someone he'd run into the evening before. "I'm always running into the same fifty people."

And Harvey, without a pause, would shoot back, "Yeah, and they've all got your insurance number by now."

They even respected each other's music—an odd assortment for a repair shop, some of it on tape, some on the radio, anything from bluegrass and country-and-western to blues and baroque, and an occasional few minutes of a program like "All Things Considered."

Bud brought in the bluegrass and country-and-western tapes. They were never played loud, but just audible enough to sing along to. Harvey brought in old show tunes, and Aretha Franklin, and Ray Charles, and the three of us spent an hour or so one afternoon singing "I'm busted" again and again along with Ray, Harvey in his deep basso, Bud using his falsetto trill, me somehow carrying the tune. "We've got the makings of a barbershop quartet," Bud said.

That was on a good day. Most days were good days. But inevitably, some were not. There were days, no matter how good you were, when things happened. Like a bike falling off the work table.

I'd been prepared for a lot of swearing in the shop. Swearing was part of it, I thought, part of the aggressive masculinity of the whole endeavor. It's a given that men doing hard physical work swear a lot—one of those images reinforced by movies and tough-guy novels.

I was also inured to swearing. In my neighborhood in Manhattan, the punk ethic combined with an overload of homeless people and junkies on the street meant that you could hear "fuck," or any of its variations, grammatical and otherwise, dozens of times in the course of walking one city block. One of the symptoms of an impoverished imagination is the adherence to a single swear word. After a while, it becomes like the pulse of the city—part of the background, something you pay no conscious attention to. Until, that is, it's not there.

It wasn't there at Just Imports. I didn't realize this until the second week. It was rather like the absence of pain: something you perceive only later, perhaps because presences are easier to register than absences.

There was the occasional off-color joke, made tentatively at first, it seemed, to see how I'd react, and then continued here and there, to be savored, groaned at, registered with mock disgust, responded to with another, worse one, perhaps, and then forgotten. Men were the targets of the jokes as much as, or more than, women.

And although neither Harvey nor Bud was a churchgoer or a believer, I sensed that they were, in fact, slightly puritan. Bud would get grossed out by some of Harvey's cruder jokes. "You're a real son of a bitch, you know," he'd say, and Harvey would smilingly agree. Other times, Harvey would be the one to be disgusted. The truth is, they were both moralists at heart. And they still accorded swear words their full force. These were not words to be used lightly. They were serious. They were only for extremes. Which is why the only time I ever heard anyone working in the shop swear was when Bud dropped that bike.

Except, that is, for myself. I also swore—once. We were working on a 1984 Renault Encore that needed a new emergency brake. Not such a complicated job: simply take off the rear drums, disconnect the cable from its connection in the middle of the chassis, just on top of the exhaust pipe, and install the new one. The only trouble was that the connection was nearly impossible to reach. The pipe itself was in the way, and there was no room to maneuver a wrench.

Finally, Harvey got to a boiling point of frustration. He stomped off to get something cool to drink in the store across the road. "Here," he said, handing me the wrenches, "see what you can do."

So I was standing alone under the car, reaching up with both arms in an effort to get a hold on the nut around the main bolt, sweating, rust and dirt in my face, working as much with my fingers as with the wrenches, and after a quarter hour or so, I'd found a frustratingly slow way of doing it, about an eighth of a turn at a time. My arms were aching, the work was dirty and tough, and just as I realized it would take me at least another ten or fifteen minutes, Carl walked by and said, "How's it going?" and I replied between gritted teeth, "This fucking Renault."

No tools dropped to the floor behind me, but there was a sudden silence from Bud's side of the shop. Carl, ever cool, just smiled and nodded in acknowledgment, as though to say that now I'd reached another stage of understanding about the mechanic's life.

That, of course, is when people really swear—in frustration. In anger. In impotence.

When you feel beaten, mystified, unable to cope, when you can't see your way through, when whatever it is you're dealing with assumes the proportions of a giant brick wall, the impulse is to swear—to swear *at* that thing, whether it be a nail, a car, a person, a bureaucracy, even the world. You want to curse it out, as though the fault lay entirely outside you, not in your own inability to deal with it. I swore at that Renault because it seemed to me that it was giving me grief. The fault was in the design, not in my lack of patience.

In fact, the fault was in both. Few cars are designed with repairs in mind. Even so simple a thing as getting hold of the oil filter can be an effort, so that when we put a Mazda up on the lift one day and I saw the oil filter right there within easy reach, I was astonished. Thought on the part of design engineers is sometimes as hard come by as patience on the part of mechanics.

There was a reason that bike fell. Accidents don't just

happen. Any race driver will tell you that. There is always a reason.

In this case, it was impatience.

The bike's owner was waiting upstairs in the office, and for some reason he was in a tear. Every half hour or so, there'd be another inquiry: Was it finished yet? How much longer?

It was the kind of pressure no mechanic likes or needs, unless of course he's working in the pits at a racetrack, where he thrives on it. It set up a troubled atmosphere around the job, so that it seemed almost inevitable when, just as it looked as though the bike was done, the kicker came loose. And this extra small job, turning up exasperatingly at the last moment, was the straw that sent the bike toppling.

Bud was trembling with anger and mortification. He paced up and down silently, tight-lipped, watching as Carl and Harvey and I cleaned up and figured out the damage to the fairing. They'd have to give a loaner to the owner, and fix the bike on the shop's time and bill. That was not the problem. The real problem was that Bud was suddenly publicly fallible. He'd lost control, lost his cool, lost his skill. His was the kind of anger only a perfectionist can feel.

Nobody was quite sure how to act with him. Not even Carl, who'd known him for years. The general consensus seemed to be that it was wisest to keep some distance: give him room to stew, pretend as though we weren't all watching him, and go back to our own jobs. But we were all unsettled and ill at ease. Somehow Bud was the one person this should not have happened to. His carefully constructed image of serene, confident capability had been toppled like the bike itself, dented and damaged. It is always hard to see a proud man mortified.

Eventually, Bud went off to get some lunch, came back with it, sat down and ate it, and all seemed to be as usual again. But when he began working on another bike, it was clear that all was not as usual. He was hurrying the job, forcing it, and as he worked he began to talk about what a terrible day it was, and how come this bolt wouldn't go in here, and why couldn't they design a bike better than this. If he didn't slow down and regain some patience, there was clearly going to be more trouble.

Bad news runs in company in a small repair shop. Once that bike had fallen, it was a hard day all round. Harvey and I were working on a 1969 Mercedes 250, putting new boots on the rear axle and a new flexidisc at the front end of the drive shaft. But the tooling of the flexidisc was off by a couple of millimeters. This is a common problem with parts. Either manufacturers bother less with quality control on parts, or they change specs on them, or sometimes simply the wrong thing gets put in the right box. Whichever way, it's a mechanic's headache, and one of the reasons why customers so often get frustrated by hearing "The part hasn't arrived yet" for the umpteenth time.

To make matters worse, Harvey had to spend the better part of the afternoon tuning the Merc, which kept stalling and then over-revving, and none of this was made any easier by the fact that the grill in this model was attached to the hood so that it hung down when the hood was open, ready to crack the head of any mechanic over four feet tall.

All this, and worse still: Harvey had met an old friend for lunch and they'd talked politics, which had gotten him worked up and angry, as it always did, about how much was being wasted on weaponry, corruption, and so on. We played no music on the cassette deck that afternoon. Nobody was interested. It was a long afternoon, and for Bud, still working as Harvey and I left, it was clearly going to be a far longer night.

A good mechanic has patience. He doesn't need to swear and curse because he's in sync with what he's doing. He's not rushing to "get this goddamn car out of here." He's taking the time the job requires. If you want your car worked on well, the moral is simple: never rush a mechanic.

There's an odd anomaly in this. The mechanic is dealing with something designed to go fast. Often, with something admired primarily for its speed. Yet he works on it slowly, methodically.

Ironically, the pace I learned in the repair shop was the antithesis of the pace I'd been going on the road. I seemed to exist simultaneously in two antithetical time frames. At speed on the road, I could enter the experience of cars from one angle, and through mechanics, from quite another. The two involved very different sets of mind. The one was slow, methodical, and careful; the other, fast, instinctive, and inherently risky.

Dealing with the machinery of rapid motion when it was at a standstill was fascinating. It was one thing to drive a powerful car; quite another to be able to *see* how it worked. There was a particular satisfaction in knowing that all the things I'd heard about—pistons, crankshafts, overhead cams, double wishbone suspensions, and so on—were real, comprehensible, touchable, manipulable. They were tangible elements in a world of logic and order and reason.

I loved how everything fit together. Every morning before work, I'd take a textbook of auto mechanics with me to the local diner, and over a working breakfast of eggs and bacon and toast, I'd study the exploded diagrams, with the parts of a clutch or a gear assembly carefully drawn and spread out in space, in the order in which they were assembled, each one with its own separate existence and importance so that a washer gained as much distinction as a gear, a pin as an output shaft.

These diagrams were based on an instructive deception, since in actuality several parts fit one over the other, bunched up together so that if you didn't already know the component parts, you'd think the piece a unified whole. Everything has its role, the diagrams seemed to say. If any one of these constituent parts should be missing, no matter how small or humble, the whole fine assembly will be in jeopardy—might even explode in chaos.

Then I'd go in to work and see those exploded diagrams become reality. I could manipulate universal joints and constant-velocity joints and watch them working. I could play with a suspension system and watch something as rigid as metal flex and stretch and bend.

Taking apart a transmission was like unlocking a door to the secret of motion. I could slowly turn the gear shafts, watch the gears connect and disconnect, admire the mind that first came up with the idea of different gear ratios. I could hold a clutch plate in my hand, and wonder at how it reminded me of a piece of sculpture by Jean Arp. Day by day, piece after piece of the car slipped into place in my mind, becoming part of a harmonious whole.

And as I worked on the machinery, aware finally of exactly how it could create motion, I began to understand how it was possible to think of the soul of a machine. The mystique of speed is bound into the metal that creates it. In a Faustian kind of bargain, we endow the metal with our own souls.

VI

I LOVED WORKING AT THE SINK. Harvey thought this was
perverse of me. He was probably right. It was one of the
dirtiest jobs in the shop.

The sink was a neatly self-enclosed system: a steel tub set
atop a barrel containing parts cleaner, a small pump suck-
ing the cleaner up from the barrel into a tube with a thick
steel brush at the end, and a filter to clean the used fluid
before it drained back into the barrel to be used again.

Working there, I'd stand with my back to everything else
in the shop, concentrated entirely on the mass of gunked
parts before me. The gunk was thick, black. The parts were
so filthy they seemed almost anonymous, just so many

interchangeable relics of the mechanical age. Even thinking of cleaning them at first seemed pointless.

But leave something to soak in that sink for a while, then come back to it and start scrubbing, and a kind of magic happened. What had been anonymous began to reveal form and personality. Vague shapes achieved particularity.

Black paled, gleamed here and there, turned slowly to silver. An ancient alchemy took place right under my hands as I hosed and scrubbed. Years of baked grease and oil and road dirt gave way to the corrosiveness of the parts cleaner, and as I worked, it seemed that here, under my very hands, I was rediscovering the original form, the bright gleaming essence of each part. Old melted gaskets disappeared under the brush. Flywheel teeth became sharp and effective. Clutch plates became intricate pieces of sculpture. I had a distinct sense of creating each part anew, of restoring its form and function.

And all the time, of course, I was breathing in the fumes of the parts cleaner, so that I am still not sure if the work itself was really that satisfying, or if I was simply so high that it seemed that way.

All the cleaners began to smell good—a seductive, chemical smell that seemed to enter my head, clear my sinuses, clean up all the synapses of my brain. There was the 5-56, so much like dry-cleaning fluid that I sometimes thought if I just stood in the path of its fumes, it would clean the clothes right on me. Oddly, I'd always hated that smell before. Then there was the Carb Clean, for gummed-up carbs; the Brakleen brakes cleaner, each can with a thin red straw laid horizontally across its black cap like the headgear of a Japanese geisha; and the Gunk—a registered trademark name for heavy-duty engine cleaner.

I had no idea just how addictive the fumes were until a few weeks into my apprenticeship, on our Monday off. I was driving past another repair shop that was open on Mondays. The windows of my car were wide open, and as I went by, I recognized the smells of parts cleaner, gasoline, lubricants—all the acids and oils with which I now worked five days a week. I slowed way down, breathed in deep, and was suffused with an immense sense of well-being.

After a month, the shop and the smells and the work were in my dreams. They were good dreams, but I'd wake with the fumes still in my nostrils, wondering how smells from a dream could spill over into the first moments of waking. Was the sense of smell independent of reality? Was my brain so addicted that it could create the smell by itself, without any external stimulus?

No matter how seductive the fumes, however, there was no doubt as to the corrosiveness of the parts cleaner: it turned my tanned hands a whitish hue and made the skin parchment dry. I began to use rubber gloves when working at the sink, but even then the chemicals seemed to work their way through the rubber, and my hands still paled.

Meanwhile, the blackened asbestos dust from the brake pads was just plain hazardous. It was caked onto the calipers and the whole of the brake assembly. Cleaning it out demanded a screwdriver and a rag and copious amounts of Brakleen. It was close-up work, so that however careful I was, I still inhaled the dust.

You take all the precautions you can in a repair shop. You keep as many doors and windows open as possible. You keep fans going. You back out cars and bikes to start them up, or if you have to start them inside, you attach a hose to the exhaust pipe and run the fumes outside. You could, of course, wear a mask, but few mechanics do. Most know they should, but the masks are hot and stuffy and they get in the way. And besides, the truth is that most mechanics do not worry about fumes. They have bigger things to worry about: a jack or a hoist giving way, a fire, a loose part spinning off. Auto mechanics is not a safe profession.

Despite all the protestations of writers and researchers that intellectual work is hard and exhausting, physical work is harder. Like anyone who's done it day in and day out, I now know this in my bones.

For years, I argued that intellectual work was exhausting, as indeed it can be. After a few hours at the typewriter, there is little I can do for a while. All my energy has been consumed, poured onto the page. Sometimes I do some physical work for a change—scythe an overgrown garden, for instance, or clean the oven. In such circumstances, physical work seems a pleasure and a relief, something that produces a healthy kind of exhaustion instead of the enervating overload of the mind that I am escaping.

This kind of short-term excursion into physical work can indeed make it seem attractive. But when you do it for a living, it exacts a heavy toll. The long-term effects of fumes and asbestos dust working their way into the body's cells are one thing, but the short term can be riskier still. With all due respect to the physical strain on hands, eyes, back, and brain from working at a keyboard all day, in physical work you can literally break your back.

I was lucky. I only sprained mine.

The culprit was a Datsun 240Z. It arrived on a truck with a note that read, "It went to Woodstock, and while there, the gears went." Just that, and a signature.

It hadn't been cruising the idyllic scenery of Woodstock. It had been drag racing. The owners had put a six-cylinder 260 engine into it, with triple carbs and a psi gauge. There'd been a big pop, it seemed, and then—nothing. No motion.

"We'll have to pull out the transmission and replace it," said Carl.

I was delighted. The heavier the work—the more it got down to the basics, into the actual drive mechanisms—the happier I was because the more I'd learn. Better still, if we had to replace the transmission, I could take the broken one apart. I already knew from the exploded diagrams in my textbook that there's nothing like taking things apart to understand how they work. Putting them back together again, I had still to discover, is yet another level of understanding.

The Z-car rode so low to the ground that we had to jack it up just to get the arms of the hydraulic lift underneath it. Harvey removed the bolt at the bottom of the transmission case so we could drain the transmission fluid—foul-smelling stuff—and found a small chunk of metal sitting on top of the bolt. "Bad sign," he said. "Something's come loose and ripped through the gears."

The next stage was to get the exhaust system off. That should have been simple enough, but there was so much gunk and rust that even after we'd loosened all the bolts, nothing moved. So Harvey stood up front and yanked, and I stood toward the back, pulling and yanking at the pipe above my head.

I felt something go inside me. Somewhere in my adbomen, it seemed. But I was focused on that exhaust pipe, eyes half-closed against flecks of grit and rust, and paid no attention. Harvey finally managed to loosen the front end, then we swapped places, me steadying as he pulled, and finally, lo and behold, the pipe slid off. We disconnected the fuel and oil lines, and then faced the really tough part.

When you're deeply involved in hard work, you simply don't notice pain. By the time we got the transmission case down from its mountings and into the yard, and then dismantled the clutch, it was late afternoon, and it was clear that this was going to be a long, drawn-out job. The drive plate and flywheel were so badly worn that they too would have to be replaced.

I went home that night exhausted. That was nothing unusual. Most evenings I'd flop down in an armchair with a beer in one hand, and find myself unable to move. It was the kind of deep exhaustion that comes only from hard physical work, the kind that you can feel in every muscle of your body, that seems to reach into your bones and sit there, making them feel both incredibly heavy and weightless at the same time. There is a strange kind of floating feeling to this exhaustion, yet at the same time you are convinced that you must weigh twice what you usually weigh.

If someone had shouted "Fire!" right then, I'd have nodded, said "Fine," and not moved an inch.

This stage of exhaustion would usually last a good half hour or so, and in that half hour, I'd hold my hands up in front of my face and wonder where all those cuts and burns and scrapes had come from. From the repair shop, obviously, but what car, what movement, what moment? I never knew. Cuts and burns and scrapes and other minor injuries were just part of the job, so much so that I never noticed them at the time. Only later, in another place and time, in a comfortable armchair as the sun was setting, did they begin to seem remarkable. And then I'd feel an odd pride in them. They were proof of my work, small badges of my apprenticeship.

That Z-car had been a tougher job than most. We'd been working on it nearly the whole of the ten-hour day, and now, as I sat still, I realized my abdomen was really hurting, and that the pain was spreading to my back. A pulled muscle, I thought. We had three days off now for the Fourth of July weekend, and I was glad: my body needed it.

The next morning, I picked up a loaded wheelbarrow of split wood, turned it to the right, and could almost swear that I heard something go pop in my lower back, just like the gears of that Z-car. For the first time in my life, I understood what crippling pain was. By the time I got to a chiropractor in Barre, the only one around who'd see me on a holiday weekend, I couldn't walk without a crutch.

Half an hour later, I walked out carrying the crutch—still in pain, but mobile. The chiro, young and gentle, merely smiled tolerantly when I compared him to Christ.

"This back has forty-eight hours to heal," I told him.

"It will probably take four or five weeks," he said.

I shook my head. "It can't," I said. "I've got to go to work."

He studied my face. "Come on in tomorrow and the next day," he said, "and we'll see what we can do."

That included the Fourth of July itself. Rob Borowske became more and more Christ-like in my mind. Forty-eight hours of cold compresses, gentle stretching, electrical stimulation, aspirin, and chiropractic adjustments did not make for the happiest of weekends, but on the morning of July 5, I was there at Just Imports, a compress strapped to my lower back, cautiously mobile.

It wasn't macho that made me so determined. Partly it was the awareness that if I lay in bed and played invalid, my back would "freeze" and take far longer to heal. But more than that, it was the knowledge that Harvey and Bud would have to literally break their backs before they'd stay away from work. A mere "subluxation" simply did not rank. Not alongside what Harvey had been through.

The back healed quickly. Between Rob's four or five weeks and my forty-eight hours, it compromised on two weeks, although by the middle of the first week I was working as I had been. Being on my feet all day helped. Besides, I had to take apart that transmission case, discovering in the process that Harvey had been right: ball bearings had come loose and torn through the gears. No wonder nothing would move.

Harvey asked after the back a couple of times, but after that it was business as usual. Neither he nor Bud nor Carl thought it at all odd that I should turn up for work. Injuries were just part of the job. My back, the left foot I bruised badly when I moved a motorcycle the wrong way, the concussion I'd get a couple of weeks later when I'd stand up and hit my head on the strut of the hydraulic lift ("Every apprentice has to do it at least once," said Harvey)—these were just par for the course. As one injury healed and another replaced it, I began to think of them as rites of passage: stages in my evolution as an apprentice.

VII

OCCASIONALLY, I'D DRIVE OVER to Barre to pick up specially tooled parts from the foundry. Barre, settled by Italian granite quarriers at the end of the nineteenth century, is still a stark redbrick contrast to Montpelier's white-shingled New England grace, even though it's just a few miles away. The foundry, Trow and Holden's, was set right by the river so that it could use the water as power. It converted to the electrical mains only in the 1960s.

The place was positively Dickensian. Workers sat in plain plastic sling seats suspended on rods from the high wooden ceiling, each in front of his own forge and trip-hammer. The noise was deafening, and when the largest trip-hammer was in operation, the vibration was so strong that the whole road outside trembled. Overhead ran the huge leather belts that drove the machinery; a little daylight came in through windows set high in the wall, but mostly this was a self-enclosed world, with the fires flickering on the faces of the workers.

It had started over a hundred years ago as a "fork factory," making agricultural implements—pitchforks and plows and parts for carts and wagons. Then, as Barre became a granite-quarrying center, the foundry went industrial, and now made pneumatic quarrying tools as well as other tools of the mechanical age. The repair shop sent brake discs there to be ground and polished, and occasionally Bud would come up with a special request for valve springs or cylinder heads to his specifications.

I loved going there. It was like returning to the roots of internal combustion, to the heat and the grind of the machine age. And more, it was a reminder that nothing could be taken for granted: not the movement of a car, nor its component parts, nor the tools with which we worked on those parts. Everything, down to the smallest bolt or shim, involved metal, and heat, and the sweat of human labor.

"Use the right tools," Harvey kept telling me. "A good mechanic uses good tools. If you don't want to damage the car—or yourself—you'd better."

The only tool that would have saved me from that back injury was experience, but as the weeks went by, I found out the hard way how right he was. After I'd sweated and puzzled at removing a snap-ring with a regular pair of pliers, and then done it a second time with snap-ring pliers and seen a thirty-minute job become a thirty-second one, I was a complete convert.

Harvey and Bud both used their own tools, assembled in bright red cabinets by their respective work stations. Both men favored Snap-On tools, which accounted for the number of Snap-On Tool-Mate thermal mugs around the shop. Out of bravado, I'd instantly adopted Danielle, Tool-Mate for July–August 1988, who posed provocatively with a torque wrench. April, who confoundingly was the Tool-Mate for July–August 1987, was clearly into impact wrenches. Like the girlie calendars that hung here and there on the shop walls, half-hidden by more recent calendars of scenery or cars, they were just part of the landscape, no longer registered except by newcomers like myself.

Snap-On tools are known for high quality—and high prices. Harvey had tens of thousands of dollars invested in that red cabinet and its contents. And going through it was like going on a mini-tour of the mechanical age.

Take just the sockets for the power wrenches, for instance. There were regular impact sockets, deep ones, and extra deep ones, plus adaptors for each one, as well as universal impact sockets. And all of these came in two sets of measurements—American and metric. A single nine-piece set neatly arranged by size in a tray cost up to $250. If you had a full complement, you owned fourteen sets.

Then there were the manual wrenches: combination wrenches, angle wrenches, open-end and combination flex-box wrenches, half-moon wrenches, tube wrenches, S-shape wrenches, ratcheting wrenches, tube wrenches, and crowfoot wrenches, as well as the many types of torque wrench. And these, also, all came in both American and metric sizes, with holders that could extend their reach, each costing anywhere up to $125.

I knew about standard and Phillips screwdrivers, of course, but I wasn't prepared for hex head and Torx head drives, let alone Pozidriv tip, carburetor tip, clutch, Robertson, magnetic, and Torx magnetic screwdrivers. Or the vast array of pliers: ignition, angle-nose gripping, self-gripping, multi-purpose, curved jaw, pipe wrench, groove-joint, slip-joint, long-nose, snap-ring, lock-ring, vise-grip, locking clamps, and chain clamps.

This is not to speak of the many kinds of power wrenches (up to $700 apiece), hammers, pneumatic tools, drill bits, dies, gauges, grease guns, picks, hooks, awls, pullers, installers, wire strippers, calipers, micrometers, pry rods, punches, and chisels. Or of the shop equipment—the battery chargers, testers and cables, creepers, droplights, diagnostic analyzers, timing lights, digital multimeters, circuit testers, compression testers, oxyacetylene equipment, alignment equipment, air compressors, bench grinders, jacks and jack stands, presses, vises and hoists, and of course the hydraulic lifts (nearly $7,000 a go).

"They've got us by the short and curlies, those tool companies," Harvey confided as we bent together under the hood of an Audi, getting ready to adjust the timing belt. "Sometimes I can't believe how expensive tools are. But the fact is, I can't resist. Every time the Snap-On representative comes round, I'm there like a kid buying a new toy."

The truth is that mechanics are fools for tools. "Most of my spare cash goes on them," Harvey admitted. "Working without good tools would be like working without grease. You just can't do it."

He straightened up and shrugged. "But you know what? Cars are getting so sophisticated now that mechanics like me won't be able to afford all the tools anymore. Only the shops will be able to afford them. Then that'll be the end of auto mechanics as we know it. The electronics boys will take over. They're already calling repair shops 'diagnostic centers' and other fancy names, and soon they'll probably be walking around in white coats like doctors. And the fancier they get, of course, the more they'll charge the customers for it. You're going to have to know electronics as well as mechanics in the future, and that's a whole different ballgame. So forget the shade-tree mechanics. They're history. In fact, maybe I am too."

And then suddenly he grinned. "The thing I can't figure," he said, "is how they're going to keep the grease off those nice white coats."

I had learned to like grease. No matter how much electronics you graft onto an internal combustion engine in the form of fuel injection, antilock brakes, automatic suspension, traction control and the like, it still can't function without this most basic tool of all. And where once I'd considered grease something to avoid if possible or clean up if not, my whole attitude toward it had undergone a one-hundred-and-eighty degree turn. Now I saw it as essential to the harmonious working of an engine.

"Fifty different kinds of grease," Harvey would say happily, and sometimes it seemed he loved every one of them.

Whether there were really exactly fifty was impossible to determine. There were so many that I lost count, and in every conceivable consistency and color—not just browns and blacks, but reds and greens and blues, even the silver of Anti-Seize lubricant, and the gold of CU-800 copper lug paste.

Much of the grease ended up on me, of course. That was fine. Once a week, on Saturday afternoons, I'd change into sweats after work and go to the Laundromat, put my work jeans and the whole week's worth of T-shirts in the machine, and be amazed at how clean they came out. And at the end of every day's work, I'd smear my hands with cornhusker's lotion, rub them, watch in fascination as the viscous white stuff turned black on my skin, and then wash it all off under the hose. Dirt became something impermanent, so that I could kneel, sit on the floor, crawl under a car, get hair, nails, clothes filthy, and none of it mattered. It was as though the more dirt I accumulated, the more I learned.

I accumulated a lot of dirt, and by the end of that summer, I was high: high on what I now knew about cars, on my newfound sense of being capable around them. I knew this was absurd—I was an adult woman feeling like a teenage boy—but I didn't care. Perhaps only an adult woman can feel such a high.

What had seemed a mystery peculiar to the male gender all these years was now revealed as a reasonable matter of mechanical cause and effect. And somehow I felt prouder of this new knowledge than I could remember ever having felt about intellectual knowledge, not because of any romance of the proletariat, but because as a woman I had never expected it. Moreover, others had not expected it for me either. And there was, as always, that undeniable delight in doing the unexpected, in finding out that I could do more than I'd thought.

Yet the one thing I thought I'd learn above all—some deeper understanding of the mystique of speed and internal combustion—remained as elusive as ever. I'd gotten into the belly of the beast, true, only to discover that the belly doesn't explain the beast.

I'd thought that understanding how cars worked would alter the experience of driving them. I'd imagined myself cruising calmly along with a clear visual sense of what was happening under the hood as I drove—pistons popping, drive shaft twirling, leaf springs bending and flexing—as though by reducing speed to its mechanical elements, I could reduce its hold on my imagination.

But all through that summer, the moment I got into a car—any car, with the one exception of that red Porsche in the yard—closed the door and started the engine, I forgot all about the mechanics. I was back on the road again, and everything I knew about *how* I was moving evaporated before the sheer momentum of the movement itself.

III

MELTDOWN

I

I COULD CLAIM THAT I had come to cars tabula rasa—a naif, an innocent, discovering the various levels of transgression inherent in speed for the first time. That would be true, and at the same time, I confess, a rather convenient lie.

It is true on one level—the discovery of speed. But there is yet another kind of transgression that causes me no delight at all, and that has been there from the very beginning. It makes me feel guilty, and for a long time I therefore did my best to ignore its voice.

This voice touches the core of how I exist in the world—of my idea of myself as in the world, as part of it and therefore responsible to and for it. None of the other levels of transgression poses any real dilemma for me. On the contrary, I enjoy them. But this one is different; this time the transgression is not against the law, or against nature, or against artificial gender lines, but against my own sense of myself.

In the late 1970s, I wrote a book of impassioned environmentalism about the desert, and still consider myself an environmentalist. The environment is important to me: I need wilderness, and find peace and solace there. So what was I doing now? How could I be so deeply involved with cars, which are a major source of pollution on this planet?

I was aware of this paradox when I first started writing about cars, but I jammed it far down in the back of my mind, giving myself up to the pleasures of speed. I knew then that it would rise up again. I was surprised only that it took so long to do so.

Working in the repair shop helped bring the issue back to the surface. I had found out how cars worked, and in the end, understood more, perhaps, than I had thought. In peeling away the mystery, I now began to realize that I had also peeled away one layer of the seductiveness.

Once entered and experienced, a forbidden zone loses something of its mystique. The challenge has been taken on, and met. I had driven as fast as I probably ever would, and even though I still liked to do it, the opportunities were becoming more limited. There were those points on my license to think of, and insurance rates, mundane details that have a way of bringing even the most enchanted mind back to earth. And once I had driven everything I wanted to drive, there didn't seem to be so much to strive for. I felt less impelled, less driven, as it were. The daemon seemed to be losing some of its hold on me so that my other self could reassert itself, regain its ability to see.

And there was now no way to avoid seeing that however harmonious the workings of an internal combustion engine might be in principle, and however willing I was to get grease all over me and enjoy the high from the fumes, cars were an environmental menace: they burned gasoline and oil, and eliminated what they didn't use in the form of what we politely call emissions.

"But how naive could you be?" someone might ask. "Surely you knew this when you began playing around with cars." And yes, of course I did. But I managed to shunt it aside to another part of my mind that was somehow divorced from actual experience, from the sensations that so excited me.

I don't think I'm alone in this. We are all capable of ignoring something we know to be true but don't really want to acknowledge. You have to be ready to see things. And the repair shop had readied me.

As though it had only just been invented, I discovered the second law of thermodynamics: there can be no such thing as an absolutely efficient internal-combustion engine, and most of the energy in it goes to waste in the form of pollution. Specifically, automotive emissions account for up to two-thirds of urban smog, and a quarter of the greenhouse gas carbon dioxide, let alone a number of others gases and particles capable of eating away paint, plastics, rubber, and human lung tissue.

I began to feel as though I were in a classic love affair turned sour. Although the first flush of infatuation was past, I had become bound up in what psychoanalysts call "the love object." And by the time I realized that the love object was perhaps not quite what I had thought—when innocent excitement began to give way to a guilty sense of dependence—love had become an addiction.

To make matters worse, this addiction was not mine alone. Any addiction is hard to stop, but all the more so when it is not merely an individual matter but a worldwide phenomenon. And when it has gone on for so long.

Still, everything remained just numbers—as statistics tend to do when you are deeply involved in denial—until one day, I came across this statement from Robert Yuhnke, counsel for the Environmental Defense Fund: "There is no more profligate use of carbon than the habit of moving two tons of steel for every one-hundred-and-sixty-pound passenger."

That did it. I needed that shift in seeing, that viewpoint of someone from Mars, as it were, looking on the habits of Earth with a curiously detached eye, to make the statistics real. Of course I knew that cars pollute. But it hadn't really occurred to me that I myself was spewing carbon into the air until I read Yuhnke's statement. To be specific, up to a quarter ton of the stuff for a brand new car like my own.

Somehow "cars" had always referred to other people's cars. To some great mass of cars "out there." Not to me. The very idea that the pollution I created was measurable, let alone in such amounts, gave me a severe jolt. The cocoon was broken.

One way or another, we all need such jolts. Reason alone just doesn't do it. The atavistic pleasure of raw power is too strong. It outweighs reason, makes it seem pale, lily-livered, overly precious.

My love for speed and power now came with a very high price attached to it. It was rather like discovering what actually happened to the animals who provided the pelts for your treasured fur coat. Or hearing about the working conditions of the South African miners who bring diamonds up to the light that makes them sparkle. Or even, perhaps, discovering that the Doctor Jekyll you love is also Mister Hyde.

The dark side of my attraction to cars had seemed somehow risqué, a matter of daring, even a tantalizing toying with the possibilities of my own life and death. But when we were talking of the life and death of a whole planet, that darkness took on another dimension all together.

I could even see it, literally, in the air. Like most people, I'd assumed that the haze that seemed to hang over most of the eastern part of the United States was natural—something to do with moisture and heat, with meteorological patterns of air flow that I hadn't bothered to understand. It had never occurred to me that the haze was artificial. And that it was caused primarily by automobile pollution.

And as though what already existed were not bad enough, it was due to get worse. Far worse. The number of cars was rising by about 4.6 percent a year—two and a half times as fast as the human population—so that by the year 2010, there could be 1.1 billion cars on this planet, more than double the number for 1990. At that rate, even with alternative fuels and new "lean-burn" engines, there was no conserving a way out of the problem.

I now had a serious dilemma: I was deeply involved with something that gave me great pleasure but was also highly destructive. It seemed to me that the only way to deal with this dilemma was to turn it into a new challenge. There had to be a way to resolve it, I thought. And that search for resolution took me next to Los Angeles, the city of all cities built for the car, and now at the forefront of a new movement to radically change it.

II

FIVE MINUTES AFTER I'D LEFT the sea-breeze clean air of my oceanfront hotel, I was traveling at fifteen miles an hour on the Santa Monica Freeway through a brown haze. Oddly, I didn't mind. I confess that I'm somewhat weird in this respect: I actually enjoy driving in Los Angeles. I'm always amazed that the freeway system works and that I can find my way around it, and the pollution seems as exotic as the frangipani and palm trees.

I have one of those maps of the city with everything in relief: hills and valleys, cliffs and mountains, and the wide white ribbons of the freeways overlaid on the landscape, circling in on themselves in elaborate knots at every major intersection. They are far more prominent on the map than they are in real life, of course, but then again maybe not: the mapmakers merely gave them an exaggerated physical importance to match their psychological one.

Just making it from one side of the city to the other always pleases me, as though I've conquered something. It's an impoverished, ultra-urban kind of pleasure, perhaps, but none the less real for that.

Still, once you know the facts of what you're doing, the pleasure is somewhat tempered. I knew that I was driving through what is often called the Super Bowl of smog, and that this month would be no different from others. In every one of them, the Los Angeles basin was suffering an oil spill as large as the disastrous 1990 one in Alaska's Prince William Sound. There it had poured into the sea from the *Exxon Valdez* tanker. Here it poured into the air through millions of tailpipes.

I had a sudden image of Icarus being brought down from the heavens by the sheer weight of oil soaked through his wings, like a seabird caught in an oil spill. I shook my head and put the thought aside, concentrating instead on where I was.

This being Los Angeles, there were plenty of exotic cars on the road. Lots of Porsche 911s, of course. Lots of every sporty, flashy, or just plain expensive car I could name, in fact. Nowhere else in the world are cars so treasured, so much a reflection of the personality. And nowhere else in the world are they so underused compared to their potential. There is simply no room, no open road, and that is why the pollution is so high. Cars pollute fifty times more in stop-and-go traffic than they do on the highway, when they cruise at a more or less constant speed and therefore at a far more efficient level of energy use. It occurred to me that, in a way, Los Angeles was the perfect automotive oxymoron: a city built for cars, being destroyed by them.

By the time I reached the San Bernadino Freeway, with the island of downtown towers poking through the haze behind me, the traffic was almost at a standstill. I watched as other drivers got busy on their car phones. It was odd: here were all these people busy talking away, using the very latest technology. Some certainly had fax machines on board. Yet they were sitting in machines that were among the most dated ones we use. Compared to the fax, the car suddenly seemed a living anachronism: a ninety-year-old mechanical contraption in an era of space-age technology.

A cartoon in a recent issue of *The New Yorker* came floating into my mind. It showed the dinosaur room of the Musuem of Natural History. At first glance, all is as usual. The pterodactyl hangs overhead, and the dinosaur skeleton sits up in that strange, almost begging, position. But in this draw-ing there is one important difference: the dinosaur sits in a skeleton car made, like its occupant, of bones.

Was this the end of an era, then? Was the internal-combustion engine finally bound for the boneyard? All rea-son said it was, but no era dies with grace, and the last thing anyone should expect of the internal-combustion engine is that it quietly depart the stage leaving little more than a few oil stains on the boards. Even as more and more people were becoming aware of pollution and of its cost, a whole new generation of gasoline supercars was being planned for production: six- and seven-hundred horsepower limited-production machines costing half a million dollars and more from makers such as Jaguar, Bugatti, and Ferrari.

Even in the affluent 1980s, when they were first conceived, the very idea of such cars seemed obscene in its insistent linkage of power and money. In the 1990s, when they were scheduled for production, you would think they could only be seen as anomalies.

Yet the hold of such cars on the imagination is immense. And not only among teenage boys and oil billionaires. I too was longing for a chance to drive them. In fact, I had moped for days when I'd had to turn down an invitation to go to England and test-drive the sole prototype of the new Jaguar car.

Not that it would have done me any good under my present circumstances. A supercar would have been as stuck in this traffic as a Yugo. I would have gotten envious looks, maybe even admiring ones—and, just as likely, resentful ones—but stuck is stuck, no matter what you're driving.

Since I had no car phone, had forgotten to bring along tapes, and could find no music I liked on the radio, I went back to thinking about the mystique of the internal-combustion engine—which is known in the industry, without any apparent irony, as ICE. The real trouble, I thought, is that so many auto engineers are themselves prisoners of the ICE mystique. Some months before, I'd attended a meeting of the Society of Automotive Engineers in Detroit, and there it had been painfully obvious. While only about thirty engineers attended a workshop on electric cars, nearly two thousand crammed into a session on the design and development of the modern Indycar, which delivers a grand maximum of 2.3 miles to the gallon.

I'd stood in the back of the hall then, staring at the rapt faces of men who I thought would have known better. And I realized that what was happening here was a kind of fantasy acting-out. These were men who worked, day in and day out, on family sedans, worrying about such details as cup holders and foolproof shifting. Men who dreamed of working on a money-no-object project such as a race car or one of the new supercars, where performance was all and everything else be damned.

Such cars, of course, are pure mystique. They have nothing to do with the way people actually drive. They are really fantasy objects, angled at the very few who can afford them. Yet not even this small financial elite would be able to drive them anywhere near their potential, since they would lack the skill, the space, and the legal freedom to do so.

That makes such cars the ultimate decadence. Owning them is all that matters. Using them is irrelevant. Power and speed are reduced to status, divorced from physical reality. In the final years of what I now came to think of as the ICE age, its grandest products would be its most useless.

What greater sign of decadence is there than this?

The traffic picked up again and I eased onto the San Gabriel River Freeway, with the air becoming still hazier as I got closer to the hills that rim Los Angeles to the east. I was used to thinking about cars in terms of the open road, but perhaps this was a better setting—that is, a more realistic one.

Gasoline cars have had a long run, but however sophisticated the marketers make them seem, attaching electronic control systems to an internal combustion engine does not change it in any fundamental way. It remains basically the same as when it was first placed in an automobile ninety years ago. Much refined, to be sure, but the same basic technology.

An old technology runs its course eventually. Even if the gasoline car were not a major source of pollution, its very outdatedness would have destined it for the junkyard sooner or later. But California had just ensured that it be sooner.

New environmental regulations adopted by the state of California early in 1990 had mandated progressively lower emissions standards beginning in 1994. But the ultimate requirement of the new regulations went much farther: two percent of all new cars would have to be ZEVs, or zero-emission vehicles, by 1998; five percent by 2001; and ten percent by 2003. The longer-term aim of the regulators was to make this fifty percent of all new cars by the year 2010, and eventually, to ban gasoline altogether.

"The die has been cast," one environmentalist had told me. "The only way to do this is by an absolutely fundamental change in the character of the auto: its propulsion system."

What was about to happen, in short, was a revolution. I thought of it as the meltdown of the ICE age. The hot technology of the internal-combustion engine would have to give way to the cool one of electricity. The electrochemical engine would replace the mechanical one.

Within a year, the California program would be under consideration by a coalition of ten northeastern states—a potential total of over one third of the American car market—and seven other states, from Florida to Washington, were thinking of following suit. The European Community planned to move toward a similar program, as did Japan, which aimed at having two hundred thousand electric cars on the road by the end of the decade.

But at that point in time, the snowball hadn't yet started to gather speed. It hadn't reached what one expert would later call "the critical mass." At that point, California was the only one, and it was all too easy for Detroit and the federal government to scoff and say "Well, it's only California, what do you expect?"

Regulations can always be overturned, critics said; I was naive to think of them as having any tangible power over real life. Did I really think that a worldwide industry, and America's largest employer, was going to totally change its product simply because California had decided so?

I did. It seemed to me inevitable. The critics were only playing for time, I thought. Public awareness of the environment had reached an all-time high. We were at the start of what some had dubbed "the green decade," and gasoline was right at the top of the green hit list.

The socially responsible side of me was high on the idea of electric cars. I wanted to believe in them. In fact, I needed to. If cars could be made clean, my dilemma would be resolved. I suppose that in a way I wanted to make some kind of atonement. I wanted to make my love respectable, as though, if it could change, I could still love it the same way.

But the daemonic side of me knew better. It was one thing to convince myself that this radical change in cars was all to the good. That was the easy part. The hard part was how I felt about it, deep down.

The daemon, it appeared, had no intention of changing. I'd thought of it as daring, but now, for the first time, I realized how very conservative it was. And how very easily threatened by change. It muttered inside me in resentful complaint. I recognized its voice. I'd heard it here and there in Detroit for years.

"Glorified golf carts," it said disdainfully.

"Wishful thinking," it said.

"Electric cars will never be able to compete with gasoline cars."

"The public will never go for them."

"Who would want to buy such a thing?"

What it didn't quite say, but what it implied, was that an electric car was a castrated car. The daemon would choose such stereotypically sexual imagery, of course. "Everything you love about cars will be gone," it said. "The noise, the vibration, the sense of raw power. How could you even imagine yourself in an electric car?"

That was exactly what I was about to find out.

III

I WAS ON MY WAY TO SEE Paul MacCready, a tall, lanky aeronautical engineer whose small R&D firm, Aero-Vironment, had led the development of the first really sophisticated electric car, General Motors' Impact. To see him, that is, and to drive the car, which had just been unveiled in prototype form. No journalist had driven it as yet. I would be the first, and this alone gave me that seductive sense of once more doing something beyond the bounds. I knew it had gone to my head: in somewhat grandiose style, I felt as though I was on my way to drive the future.

MacCready is not the kind of man I would ever have expected GM to trust farther than they could see: far too iconoclastic, I would have thought, for a major American corporation. But then a healthy dose of iconoclasm is precisely what is needed to break out of a rut and imagine a different future.

A three-time U.S. national soaring champion, MacCready had designed a series of human- and solar-powered planes in the late 1970s, as well as the self-propelled, 70-pound Bionic Bat. Then, in what seemed the height of eccentricity, he built a huge radio-controlled, wing-flapping, flying replica of the largest animal ever to have flown—the long extinct *Quetzalcoatlus northropi*, or pterodactyl, with a thirty-six-foot wingspan. That, he said, was to show the connection between biological flight and technological flight.

At first all this made him sound like a mad scientist out of a movie like *Back to the Future*. It took a while to realize that such an attitude said more about how conventional my view of science had become than about the man himself. In fact, the MacCready I would meet is a restrained, cerebral, intensely practical engineer with a doctorate in aeronautics from CalTech and a long string of awards and honors. The word *genius* is used about him with what becomes exasperating frequency. There are no less than five AeroVironment inventions in the Smithsonian collection, including the Gossamer Condor human-powered plane and the Sunraycer solar car, which MacCready and his team designed for GM and which had turned in a record-breaking performance in the first World Solar Challenge Race in Australia in 1987.

After the Sunraycer's success, GM cannily bought up 15 percent of AeroVironment and gave MacCready's team the go-ahead to develop an electric car. They were apparently thinking of it primarily as a show car, but the MacCready team promptly called their bluff. In just under a year, they developed a car with a top speed of over one hundred miles an hour and a 0–60 time of eight seconds.

Most electric cars proposed in the past twenty years had been conversions of production gasoline cars. They worked, but not very well. MacCready's innovation was to apply a systems approach: by rethinking the car literally from the ground up, his team transformed the electric car from a mechanical oddity into a stylish practicality.

In fact, they literally reinvented the wheels: made out of aluminum, with tires specially designed to reduce drag, they helped make the Impact so energy-efficient that if it were to run on gasoline, it would use only one-third the amount required by a typical internal-combustion car. Even the heat generated in braking was not allowed to go to waste: in a process known as regenerative braking— "regen" for short— that energy was fed back into the batteries, recharging them.

The Impact would not have been possible without the experience MacCready's team had gained in developing the solar Sunraycer car. And that was the context in which I'd first met the man—not in Los Angeles, but on the other side of the world, where he was acting as a kind of eminence grise behind the second World Solar Challenge Race.

It had been one thing to go as far as Vermont in pursuit of knowledge about cars. Even as far as Los Angeles. But when I found myself in Darwin, on Australia's north coast, I did begin to wonder, finally, if I had not gone too far.

Darwin is the kind of place that will make you think such things.

The climate has a lot to do with that. It was very hot and very humid—the close tropical heat that precedes the monsoon season. In this part of the world, that can lead to strange behavior, anything from a simple disinclination to get out of bed in the morning to a murderous rampage. "Going troppo," they call it.

I understood the principle perfectly. It took four days to get everything ready for the solar race—four days in which I watched as the organizers checked and sealed the cars, registered the drivers and the support teams, ran safety and speed tests on a small racetrack just outside town. Four days in which everyone's nerves—those of the teams, the organizers, and the journalists—seemed to be stretched to the limit.

Finally, on the fifth day, the cars lined up on the promenade, with the Arafura Sea lapping at the beach and the palm trees swaying slightly and a large crowd milling about, waiting for the start. Children waved Australian flags; the drivers, suited and helmeted, climbed into their cockpits; the crews and engineers stood back; the photographers took last-minute shots.

Every car on the grid that morning in November 1990 was an electric car powered solely by the sun. A ridiculous, impossible feat, it seemed, yet here they were, and even though they were tangibly real, I couldn't help feeling that Darwin's waterfront had been turned into a Hollywood back lot.

Some of the cars looked as though they'd been designed for a James Bond movie in the making. Others could have come out of the last Mad Max movie. And yet others were like futuristic insects from a sci-fi movie, their huge, shiny silicon wings folded back on themselves.

Still, these things could move. I'd seen the five-million-dollar Honda car do seventy-one miles an hour in testing. I'd watched as the Mazda car, a three-pronged black and red blob using amorphous instead of crystalline silicon, swished through its time trials like some creature from outer space on hidden wheels. The Swiss car from the University of Biel was a psychedelic swirl of pink and green and blue, advertising its sponsor, Swatch watches. And five cars from American universities, all sponsored by General Motors, were almost clones of the Sunraycer.

That car alone had made MacCready a kind of icon of the solar-energy movement. But now that the prototype Impact had made its debut, his status with everyone on the starting grid that morning seemed to be something very close to God. And like God, he wasn't saying much. As we stood together on a hotel terrace overlooking the start, he told me he was there merely as an observer, and was determined to keep a low profile. I suspected that the climate didn't sit too well with him. Let alone playing God.

"Gentlemen, start your engines," went the traditional cry— even though some of the drivers were women—and there was a moment where everyone held their breath in anticipation. Then, instead of the roar of engines, there was a low hum in the air as one by one, the drivers switched on their machines. The flag went down . . . but instead of roaring out of town, the cars quietly floated out, southward-bound toward the desert outback of a country the size of the lower forty-eight American states.

The course was the Stuart Highway—known, appropriately, as The Track—an arrow-straight two-lane blacktop stretching into shimmering lakes of heat which is the only paved road running north to south through the middle of Australia. The cars would race from eight o'clock in the morning to five in the afternoon. Wherever they were at five, there they would stop, and the crews would camp overnight by the side of the road.

I hadn't expected to get emotionally involved in this. After all, it wasn't a "proper" race. Where was the heady smell of exhaust? Of burned rubber and gasoline? Where was the magnificent roar of the crowd, or of the engines? This looked like it would be just an interesting exercise in the possible. But there is something about a race—any race, even one between a tortoise and a hare—that gets the emotions involved. And as I followed the solar cars down The Track, through a desert increasingly barren and thus more and more enchanting as we went farther south, I found myself caught in one of those odd juxtapositions of time and place that catch the unwary traveler.

A couple of years before, I had been involved in another strange event: a tugboat race in the waters off Seattle harbor. Thinking about the misty setting of Puget Sound as I drove under the burning sun of the outback seemed absurd at first, and yet it made a certain kind of sense. I'd been along for the ride on one of the tugboats, and stood on the bridge with the skipper as we started off in first place. He was shaking his head in perplexed amusement at the whole thing. "I don't know why I'm getting so excited," he'd said. "We're in the lead now, but I know the capacities of every one of these boats, and I can tell you exactly how this race is going to develop. We have great acceleration, that's true, but our top speed isn't high enough to win, so by my reckoning we'll come in fourth. I know all this, so tell me, why is my adrenaline up and why am I behaving like we have a chance to win?"

Sure enough, we came in fourth. But races clearly have a way of working on the human imagination, and now, as the solar cars spread out along The Track in the ensuing days, I sped in my rental car from one camp to another in the evenings, eager to check on progress as the sun lowered. I had to keep a wary eye out for road kill—not the deer I was used to from American highways, but kangaroos and cattle, victims of the huge triple-trailer "road-train" trucks for which the road had been built. Occasionally, I'd see a line of kangaroos bounding along the top of a ridge, and if I was lucky, herds of wild camels, flocks of cockatoos and parrots, emus bounding into the bush, and once, magically, even a herd of huge wild horses slowly, very slowly, crossing the road in front of me, looking to neither left nor right, paying no heed at all to me or my car. They were like mythical creatures from another era, with the monumental grace of dignity.

By the second evening, the Honda car, the odds-on favorite, had hit trouble. Its engineers had to take the car apart at the side of the road. I watched, fascinated: there was practically nothing inside it. Underneath the solar canopy, now tilted toward the dying sun, there was no mass of metal, no jumble of steel and tubing, but the simplicity of two small electric motors, one on each of the front wheels, two stacks of lightweight silver-zinc batteries, and two small aluminum boxes housing the inverters to transform the electric charge from direct to alternating current. And that was it. Instead of pistons and grease, just boxes and wires.

The Japanese engineers worked quickly and quietly in their white overalls, and I smiled as here, at the other side of the world, I remembered Harvey predicting that the boys in the white coats would take over. I made a mental note to call him when I got back to the States and tell him there was no need to worry about the grease spoiling the whiteness. The Honda overalls were specklessly clean; there was nothing to make them dirty.

It took five days for the winner to cross the finish line south of Adelaide—a total of just over forty-six hours of actual racing time. The Honda car recovered, but the Swiss car from Biel edged it out, with a final time just slightly slower than the Sunraycer's time three years before. That didn't sound like much of an advance until I realized that the Sunraycer had used expensive space-program gallium arsenide solar cells costing over a million dollars, whereas the Swiss car used high-efficiency laser-grooved silicon cells costing twenty thousand dollars. It ran just as fast, but at a fraction of the cost.

The race was over, but despite its success, few of those who had taken part in it expected solar cars to replace gasoline cars in anything like the near future. That's not why Paul MacCready was there. It's also not why Honda, Nissan, Mazda, and General Motors were there, or why Volkswagen, Ford, Daimler-Benz, and other major automakers had given technical help and back-up to many of the teams. The fact is that the solar cars charging their batteries in the Australian sun were not, as might seem at first, mere well-meaning gestures of environmental idealism, but mobile labs of advanced electric technology representing hundreds of millions of research-and-development dollars.

This was a high-stakes race for the future. And these solar cars were research vehicles for the development of a whole new era in automotive technology. The solar race was one thing. The real race was taking place in automakers' R&D departments the world over. It was a race to determine the future of the car, and Paul MacCready was in the forefront of it. I'd lost track of him as the solar race had spread out through the desert. Now, in the Los Angeles suburb of Monrovia, I caught up with him again.

In Australia, I had thought MacCready a shy man. Like most engineers, he had seemed almost uncomfortable with words. But back in his own office, with a scale model of the pterodactyl's head hanging high on one wall like some kind of hunting trophy, he was downright voluble.

"This decade is going to be the most exciting ever in cars," he declared. "It's going to be somewhat like the thirties in aviation, when we went from canvas and sticks to airliners and fighters in just a few years."

I wasn't at all enthusiastic about the fighters, but then enthusiasm is not what MacCready is about. When he makes a statement like this one, you have to take it seriously: it comes from a pragmatic assessment of the field, not from wishful thinking.

The key, he explained, was efficiency. "To design the Impact, we had to rethink the whole question of automotive design from the point of view of efficiency, the way it's pursued in the aerospace industry. And the odd thing is that nobody had ever looked at a car from this point of view before. That sounds amazing, but there'd never been any need to. There was an 'it-works-so-don't-mess-with-it' attitude."

Working on small human- and solar-powered vehicles in the past had given him the ability to cut through the accepted wisdom of the car world and carve out a radically new path. But the determining factor in making that path a mainstream one, he said, was not technology but cost: "Economics underlies this whole issue. Cars are not airplanes. You have to make them affordable. The challenge is how to get some of the efficiency of the culture of aviation into the mass-market car culture, which is all the trickier when gasoline is cheaper in America than bottled water."

"You sound more like a Sierra Club associate than a GM one," I said.

"It simply makes sense," he replied. "The fact is that if some fearless politician with enough charisma to carry it off could introduce a slowly rising tax on gasoline to, say, four dollars a gallon by the end of the decade, the national debt would be pretty much taken care of, the economy would be revitalized, everyone's health would be better, and we'd be free of dependence on foreign oil.

"But this is America, and it's not going to happen. The fact is that when you look at problems that you think are technical, eventually you find out that they're institutional and political and societal. Technologically, there are many things we can do to make environmentally desirable cars that solve the dependence on foreign oil. They're all perfectly feasible. The question is getting them onto the market. Right now, that's being driven, so to speak, by regulations, in California and the Northeast and probably more states to follow. But I'm convinced that by 2005, electric-drive cars will win out not because of some regulation, but because they'll be better and cheaper than gasoline cars."

I hadn't expected this. I was used to auto engineers being car enthusiasts: men—and a few women—who were so deeply steeped in the ICE mystique that all they thought about, basically, was power. But here was a man who had been led into autos not by a need for speed but by a deep and abiding concern for the planet, an engineer who talked pessimistically about the rate at which species were being made extinct, who saw a "window" of thirty years in which something could still be done to turn things around and was determined to use that window to its fullest. Here, in short, was a man who might be able to resolve my dilemma.

Not that it even interested him. When I explained it, he just gave a thin smile, and in a perfectly low-key, slightly sardonic manner, effectively put down the prevailing obsession with energy-expensive, high-powered cars: "If you look at birds like the albatross, you'll see they can spend days soaring over the ocean, with magnificent maneuverability. Then at the other end of the spectrum, there's the peacock, stuck on the ground, flying at most up to a low branch. The mechanical part of a peacock's flying function is minimal, so much effort goes into other things like the large tail, which hampers flying, but boy does it make the females quiver."

The Impact had made a lot of auto journalists quiver, a thing they normally do only for peacock cars. The performance figures alone had turned their heads. MacCready's team had created the automotive equivalent of a peacock that could fly like an albatross, proving, as MacCready said, that "styling and efficiency don't have to be incompatible." And the very fact of the car's existence had undoubtedly influenced California's decision to go ahead with electric-vehicle regulations. MacCready had demonstrated quite clearly that the technology already existed.

And now I was going to get to drive the Impact. I admit, the very idea of it made me quiver too. And not entirely with pleasure. I knew that electricity would alter the experience of driving. It would make it smoother, more sophisticated, and rationally, that was probably a good thing. But reason doesn't account for everything. Some part of me looked on this sculpted, silver prototype with a jaundiced eye, as though it were some kind of rival. The excitement, I felt somehow, was more in the idea of the car than in its reality.

In the workshop, its swooping, aerodynamic lines made it look like a rather futuristic design exercise. I could easily have thought it just another flashy concept car, the kind designed to draw the crowd's attention at auto shows, but the moment I slid behind the wheel, I knew that I was in for something very different.

There was a long, disorienting moment of confusion as it suddenly dawned on me how much I take for granted in the design of a car, and how resistant I was to any sign of change. So many of the cues I was used to in gasoline cars were missing or subtly different. There was no gear shift for one thing, because there was no clutch and no transmission. Just two small electric motors, one for each of the front wheels. A long hump down the center floor of the car looked rather like the one in old sports cars, and the fact that there was a line of thirty-two lead-acid batteries under the hump instead of a drive shaft seemed the least of my worries at that moment. I was still trying to take in the dials, which were centered just below the steeply raked windshield.

Motor temperature, check. Miles per hour, fine. But then there was a dial for battery charge, marked in percentages. And another, the ammeter, marked in amps. Driving this car, I realized, would require a different frame of mind.

I turned the key, and nothing seemed to happen. No sound, no vibration. Then I pressed a button marked F for forward, put my foot down on what I couldn't help thinking of as the gas pedal, and in the ensuing silence was amazed that the car moved. It felt strangely unreal, almost eerie.

I drove slowly out of the workshop and turned onto the road. "All right, then," I thought, "let's see what it can really do." The next thing I knew, I was being pushed back into my seat by the force of acceleration. Before I quite realized what was happening, I had done zero to sixty miles an hour faster than in a Mazda MX-5 Miata.

I hadn't expected this. I felt myself smiling—that old half-smile. Until that moment, the very idea of a sexy electric car had seemed an oxymoron. But here was one deliberately designed to break the conceptual mold of electric cars as either glorified golf carts or impractical sci-fi fantasies. Here was one that might not sound like a sports car but certainly behaved like one.

Could it be that I hadn't come in at the end of an era, as I'd feared, but at the start of a new one instead? Flush with hope, I set to finding out more.

IV

IN THE REPAIR SHOP, the electrical system had been the last thing I'd attempted to tackle. "Spaghetti," Harvey had derisively called the bundles of wires bunched up behind the lights and trailing through the engine compartment. "Here," thrusting the manual at me, "you read the wiring system."

So I'd learned to read the wires—not so difficult, as it turned out, since all I had to do was follow the different colors. But even so, I was aware that although I could trace a wire to a connection, clean it, and fix it, I still had no idea how it worked. And books were no help. I'd sought out a textbook on electricity, and found this encouraging first sentence: "Nobody really knows how electricity works."

"Great," I thought, and put the book aside. After all, the electrical system wasn't the heart and soul of the car. That was the engine and the drivetrain, and they were comfortingly mechanical. That is, I understood how they worked.

But now it seemed a kind of insult that after all that effort, I was still faced with a car that I didn't understand. I felt a kind of irritation, both at electric cars and at myself, and set about learning how they worked. If this was to be the future—as I hoped it would, despite the murmurs of the daemon—then damn it, I'd be there. I'd drown the daemon with the force of knowledge.

That was easier said than done. For a time, I felt as though I were back in high school. Vague memories of long-forgotten chemistry and physics classes came floating up as I began to talk to more people about electric cars. Talking wasn't so bad—I could delude myself for a while that I understood what they were saying. Reading the papers they gave me was something else.

I was confronted by a virtual panoply of possibilities for batteries, and introduced to the idea of energy—all energy—as a chemical interchange. "It's quite simple," said one engineer almost gaily, "once you realize that electricity is just a chemical process."

I nodded as though he were right. Quite simple. If you understand chemical processes, that is. I'd last studied chemistry when I was sixteen. But now I began again.

As a journalist, I had considerably more incentive to understand than as an unwilling high-school student, and better access to instruction too. I roamed the electric-vehicle R&D sections of automakers, poking my head under the hood and inside laboratories whenever I could, asking dumb questions and getting intelligent answers. And as time went by, I actually began to understand electrochemistry. Those months in the repair shop helped with that: I had the confidence that what had formerly been mysterious could be made comprehensible once I could see, touch, and get a physical sense of how things worked.

Electrolytes and catalysts fell into place. The relative virtues and vices of lead-acid, sodium-sulfur, aluminum-air, nickel-cadmium, zinc-air, lithium-polymer, and a host of other battery combinations began to line up in some sort of orderly array in my mind. I found myself using what I came to think of as electro-speak: a whole new vocabulary that comes into being once you start thinking about electric cars instead of gasoline ones. Electric vehicles became EVs, nickel-cadmium became Ni-Cad, fuel-cell vehicles became FCVs.

And then came the day when I picked up a technical paper on hydrogen fuel that I'd put aside a year or so before as utterly incomprehensible. Now I read it straight through, nodding in sage agreement. Only when I'd finished it did I realize that I had understood every word of something that had previously been technical mumbo-jumbo.

As in the repair shop, technology was being demystified, revealed as a comprehensible matter of cause and effect, a series of logical connections that gave rise to "Yes, I see" instead of blank stares of incomprehension. I felt as though I had broken a new code.

I had to understand batteries, because they are the one factor that has held up the development of a modern electric car. In fact, the phrase most often used about them is "the Achilles heel" of electric-car development.

Hearing engineers talk about Achilles in one breath and depth of electrical charge in another is one of those odd disjunctions that happen when you're on the verge of a whole new technology. I don't know how many of the men who used this phrase knew the whole story of Achilles—just as assuredly few of those who named the early cars phaetons had any real idea of who Phaeton was—but the phrase was peculiarly apt. Achilles, the hero of Homer's *Iliad*, was the Greek ideal of courage and beauty, dipped by his mother as an infant in the River Styx to render him invulnerable—except, of course, for the one part of him that remained in contact with her and therefore untouched by the magic waters: his right heel.

True, the lead-acid batteries in the Impact produced nearly twice the energy per pound weight of regular car batteries— "We think our battery people sneaked some kryptonite in there," joked one of the engineers working on the production model—and recharged in only three hours. That was incredibly fast for any kind of battery, but it was still two hours and fifty-seven minutes too long when compared to the "recharge" time for gasoline.

Moreover, the Impact batteries would have to be replaced every couple of years. So what was needed was something that didn't yet exist: a small, compact battery with high power density, quick recharge time, and a long life cycle, using non-toxic or easily recyclable materials. And, of course, inexpensive.

"The trick now," MacCready had said, "is to come up with a real crackerjack battery."

That looked like it would have to be some trick. In 1991, Nissan announced a "super-quick charge" prototype electric car with nickel-cadmium batteries that recharged in a mere fifteen minutes. What they did not emphasize, however, was that this was at 440 volts, which is way beyond household capacity. Moreover, all indications were that the Nissan battery wouldn't have a very long life. And cadmium is highly toxic. Nissan had stretched the envelope, but they still hadn't burst through it.

Yet there seemed to be an extraordinary confidence within what had suddenly become the electric-car industry that "the" battery would be found by the magic year 1998, when the new legislation would begin to kick in. It sounded far enough away at first, until you stopped a moment and thought: only seven years, only six, only five. . . . And the year 2003 seemed impossibly far off—another century—until again you stopped to think: only eleven years, ten, nine. . . . Unless the regulations were changed, and the deadlines delayed, a whole new technology was going to have to be developed within one decade.

What made things all the stranger was that even as automakers' advanced-technology staffs were racing to come up with the next era of cars, they were still marketing gasoline cars as though they were the most sophisticated things on four wheels. It was an extraordinary kind of willed schizophrenia, all the easier to perpetrate as the public remained largely unaware both of the stakes and the race to earn them.

Inevitably, I found myself part of that schizophrenia, bouncing between technologies like some sort of time-capsule callgirl. But it was becoming increasingly hard to smile about the latest gasoline cars. Even as Chrysler were testing their TEVan, a sophisticated electric delivery van, they launched the Viper, that expensive throwback to the muscle cars of the 1960s whose prototype had so bewitched auto journalists in Sedona, Arizona, a couple of years earlier. Yet something had changed. Although most of the auto press raved as it always does about such cars, there were some voices raised in criticism. Environmental groups and even a few industry people questioned aloud the purpose and sense of the Viper. With a recession in full sway, the market for expensive cars had plummeted. And with the emphasis increasingly on cleaner cars, what was the point of a car like this?

I hadn't been sure at first whether my pursuit of electric cars was sanity, optimism, or mere wishful thinking on my part—or perhaps a combination of all three. But as time went by and more states either adopted or were considering the California program introducing zero-emission vehicles, it began to seem that somehow, extraordinarily, the right thing was finally being done for the right reasons.

And yet somehow, I was not as wholeheartedly pleased about this as I wanted to be. The various scenarios for an electric-car future failed to excite me. They seemed almost too clean, too antiseptic, too divorced from that visceral experience that had come to mean motion and speed for me.

I tried to work up some enthusiasm about the idea of hooking into a highway electronically, moving over electromagnetic strips embedded in the surface, but all I could think of was a conveyor belt. The principle of it made sense, especially if you've ever been stuck on the Long Island Expressway or any of the Los Angeles freeways. The strips would not only recharge an electric car as it passed over them, but also control its speed, steering, and distance from other cars. All the driver would have to do would be to tune into the traffic-control computer and drop out—go to sleep, program the computer to set off an alarm when the car was close to the required exit, and then drive on home on a fully recharged battery pack.

But sense isn't everything. The truth is also that such a scenario is boring. Who could get excited over it except someone who doesn't like to drive?

Solar power seemed to offer more. A kind of lodestar of the technological imagination, it tempted and tantalized with the promise of free, clean, safe energy. But it wasn't that simple. Those solar cars racing through the Australian outback had been marvels of ingenuity and determination, but they were as far removed from practical application to everyday cars as is a jetliner from a kit plane.

Solar power could be used, however, to generate hydrogen, the space-age fuel par excellence, by electrolyzing water—splitting it with an electrical charge into hydrogen and oxygen. Hydrogen can be burned in an internal-combustion engine, but a far cleaner way to use it, although still some way from market application, would be in an on-board fuel cell, which separates out the electrons in the hydrogen to produce electricity. A hydrogen fuel cell could take an electric car three times farther than an internal-combustion car on the same amount of fuel. In fact, it could take an electric car like the Impact four hundred miles on one charge.

Fuel cell technology could thus produce an absolutely clean car—one running, basically, on sun and water. It seems like the ideal solution. And within the next ten or fifteen years, it may even be on the road.

But as much as I want such a thing intellectually, it still sounds almost suspect, as though it were somehow against the very nature of the beast. Or more precisely, as though it were taming the beast. Which is exactly its purpose.

Something in me, wary of domestication, wants to protest this. If the beast is tamed, its very nature will change, and we will lose some essential element of automotive movement. Yet isn't this what was said when typewriters began to replace the pen, and again when personal computers began to replace the typewriter? At each stage, we feared that the new technology would take us away from some inner essence of the writing process, as though the essence were in the mechanics instead of in the head. At each stage, as we have and probably always will do, we confused ourselves with the tools we use.

And yet again. . . . I began to argue with myself, back and forth, the two sides of me struggling for ascendancy. The tools we use are part of us. They determine how we approach our work, or our pleasures. Even the most devoted user of word processors will admit, in a weak moment, that there is some lack of intimacy with what we still call the written word. How we do something is part of the result. The means do shape the ends, and the shape of the word, as formed by the hand, is different from, more palpable than, its printed appearance on the screen.

Where mechanics allows for some intimacy with the engine, some tensile feel for steel and iron, for power and pressure and strength, electrochemistry makes everything more remote. Unless you are Thomas Edison, it is hard to feel intimate with electricity.

True, the speed itself will still be there with electric cars. Eventually, they will probably go even faster than gasoline cars. But there won't be that combustive force of the mechanical engine. There won't be the heat, the vibration, the roar of an engine at high revs. It is almost as though speed will exist independently of the driver, as a cold measure, a mere figure on the dial achieved too effortlessly to be truly felt.

The visual cues of speed will still exist, to be sure, as will the g-force, but everything else will be missing. It will be rather like hearing a piano concerto without the orchestra: the essential element—the piano—will play, but the piece as a whole will lack the tonality, the richness, the harmony with which it was conceived. It will become more of an intellectual experience, divorced from emotion.

And that, I tried to persuade myself, was all to the good. Electric cars would indeed be better, as MacCready had said. They made sense.

But what then would become of the daemon?

V

I SUPPOSE IT WAS INEVITABLE that I would drive the Deux Chevaux again. It was a risky thing to do, I knew. How would memory stand up to my experience of the past few years? How would twenty-eight horsepower feel after four hundred?

It can be downright dangerous to put nostalgia to the test of experience. That way lies disappointment. And I probably would not have attempted it were it not for two intriguing facts.

The first was that General Motors' Advanced Technology Center, home of the company's electric-car development effort, had been checking out the Deux Chevaux as an example of a lightweight car with a distinctly unpowerful engine that had nevertheless provided safe and reliable transport for longer than most of the bright young engineers in GM's Tech Center had been alive.

The second was Chrysler's development of a new concept car, the Dodge Neon. Concept cars are vehicles that engineers and designers have dreamed up, sometimes seemingly right out of the blue, and that may or may not go into production in much toned-down form at some point in the future. Also known as dream cars or blue-sky cars, they are the attention-getters of auto shows. But this one got the attention of professionals too. The two-stroke engined Neon won the industrial designers' gold excellence award for innovation that year. Yet it was distinctly familiar. Tiny and lightweight, with a humped profile, a canvas roll-back top, and canvas seats slung on an aluminum frame, it was unmistakably a modernistic interpretation of the Deux Chevaux.

These two facts were my rationalizations. The truth was simpler: I couldn't resist. I'd heard that a small firm in Toronto was rebuilding Deux Chevauxs from the chassis on up, so I called Canada, and a few weeks later there I was, clutching the keys to a funkily elegant Charleston model painted with a big maroon swirl on black.

I have clutched the keys to just about every car in the average teenage boy's pantheon of dream cars, but I don't think the prospect of driving any one of them ever made me so plain happy as did the prospect of driving the Deux Chevaux again. Now that I saw it once more in the flesh, as it were, all my worries dissipated. This was one of those rare times when reality and memory meet and embrace. Later they told me that I was literally dancing with anticipation.

The moment I turned on the ignition, everything came back in a rush. And as I maneuvered through the streets of Toronto toward the outskirts of the city, I realized that what was so evocative—more even than the look of the car or the feel of it—was the sound of it.

I had listened to engineers explaining how they adjust the exhaust pipes on sports cars to produce the perfect exhaust note, but I'd never realized before just how primary sounds are in identifying a car—and in identifying with it. Here, there was the persistent putter of the engine, the whistle of air through the vents, the flap of the canvas roof once I got up to fifty miles an hour. And every sound conveyed information. I drove the car on sound. My ears brought back the memory of precisely when to change gears for the highest power. And all those years between now and then simply slipped away.

The Deux Chevaux was still a defiantly simple pleasure. People in other cars smiled and waved. It made them happy. And me too. I could *feel* the machinery, and this made mobility interesting again, involving, with something of that old memory of the very first time I put my foot on a gas pedal—the delight in having something mechanical move me at will. I could feel how this car moved me physically, and therefore it moved me emotionally and intellectually too.

And yet as I headed up into the hills north of Toronto, I knew how old-fashioned of me this was. Most high-tech modern cars—the Lexus, the Infiniti, the Mercedes-Benz— were deliberately designed to break the combustive bond between physical and emotional movement. They were so well insulated that you could put Glenn Gould playing Bach's Goldberg Variations on the stereo system and still hear him humming in the background. The Deux Chevaux, however, had no stereo; it made too much noise. In its own homely way, it was as much a relic of the hot combustive era of cars as the latest Ferrari or Lamborghini.

It was a nice coincidence that I thought all this as I was driving through the territory of Marshall MacLuhan, the Canadian Merlin of cool. Not long after, I re-read his classic *Understanding Media*, with its explanation of hot and cool:

"A hot medium is one that extends a single sense in 'high definition.' High definition is the state of being well filled with data. . . .Telephone is a cool medium, or one of low definition, because the ear is given a meager amount of information. . . . Hot media do not leave so much to be filled or completed by the audience."

What this means is that hot takes over, cool does not. Right now we seem to be on the verge of what MacLuhan called "a break boundary" in our concept of power—from a hot, physical concept of it to a cool, post-modernist one. Clark Kent has become the real superman, not the guy in the fancy costume. Slim Robocop outperforms muscular Rambo. The jazz, hip meaning of cool is back, in the sense of laid-back, and cultural icons have merely followed the style of technological developments: the passage from typewriters to computers, from hot-metal printing to desktop publishing, from scalpel surgery to laser surgery, iron to aluminum, cash to plastic.

All these developments approximate their predecessors in their effects, but work in radically different ways. The computer produces typed writing, as did a manual typewriter. The result remains the same; the way it is achieved is on another order of technology.

And now cars appear to be on the brink of a break boundary on a similar order of magnitude. The combustion engine, with images of oily hands, roaring exhausts, and the heady smell of burning gasoline, could take over the senses. It was hot. But the efficiency of electrochemistry does not involve the senses in the same way. The electric car is cool.

I have no doubt that a new mystique will be built around it to replace the hot combustive one. Raw power will give way to calm sophistication, and what was visceral will become cerebral. It has already begun in luxury gasoline cars; the electric car will take it farther. The very idea of the car, it seems, will become more rational.

And there, of course, lies the rub.

The daemon detests rationality. By its nature, it is hot, fiery, consuming. It is a creature of passion, not of reason, and it seems to contain some essential part of me. If it were to be lost in the transfer from a hot to a cool technology, something in me too would then be lost.

Suddenly, I find myself wanting to protect the daemon. I've always thought of it as strong, as something that impels me, almost against my own wishes. But now that it is under threat, I see how much I need it. I couldn't tolerate its becoming just a memory of another time, like a youthful affair viewed from the perspective of a stable married life.

Perhaps, eventually, high technology will evoke as much passion in me as low. For some, I know it already can. There is the science-fiction world of William Gibson's cult cyberpunk novel *Neuromancer*, in which physical reality is superseded by virtual reality. Adventure and sensation lie not in physical movement but in the movement of the mind through the connections and synapses of cybernetics. The novel is a vision of the future based on a blending of self with machine on a far higher order than driving. A future so cool that, like hot ice, it burns.

The trouble is that I have never been good at cool. I have always envied those who are. They seem so much more in control of themselves, so much less vulnerable to the vicissitudes of impulse and emotion. Where I dance up and down in excitement, they nod sagely, giving a restrained approval all the more sought after for being so hard to evoke.

Still, cool or hot, Gibson's world and mine have one vital element in common: that desire to expand the limits of human movement. I speed on the road; Gibson's characters speed through cyberspace. But whether we have a steering wheel or a computer keyboard beneath our hands, the basic impulse is the same. It is the addictive excitement of transgression.

The daemonic soul, then, lies in movement, not in the means of it. And the essence of the car lies not in what is under the hood but in the head of the person driving it. It is the very idea of motion, and the sensation of it. This is the true content of auto-mobility. Not in the metal, but in the eyes, the hands, the mind, the innards—even the soul—of the driver.

It seems that no matter how sophisticated or simple the means, the basic need for motion, for breaking through barriers and boundaries, is an atavistic one, perhaps even an evolutionary one. It may be some essential spark of life itself. And strive as we might to be rational creatures, to limit our imaginations and ambitions and to live calmly and evenly, we somehow diminish ourselves if we attain that goal. There will always be further realms, always more room in an infinite universe for transgression. Human movement will never be able to keep up with the human imagination, and in the space created by that disparity, the daemon roams and plays, constantly beckoning us beyond our limits.

It has led me many times into places I never imagined I would venture: into deserts and up mountains, onto podiums and around racetracks. And now, in reaction to the coming era of sanity in cars, it beckons again.

"Look up," it says. "Think of a freedom of motion you've never experienced before. Imagine speed in three dimensions instead of two."

I looked up into a wide blue sky, and laughed. "But of course!" I thought. It was so easy to imagine in a fast car that I could fly. Why not actually do it? And if the shades of Icarus and Phaeton flickered across that vast expanse of sky, so much the better. What kind of daemonic impulse would involve no risk?

The daemon is indomitable, and no matter what, I am grateful for it. There will always be another dimension in which it will find expression. It beckons; I follow. After all, what would life be without it?

ACKNOWLEDGMENTS

My thanks to the many people who have aided and abetted me in my metamorphosis into a fast woman, and especially to Valerie Klabouch, who first said "You should write a column about cars"; to Gael Love, who called that column "Carnal Knowledge"; to my friends and colleagues in the International Motor Press Association, who answered my questions without laughing (most of the time, at least); to Carl and Janice von Schummer, who were brave enough to allow me to work in their repair shop; to the MacDowell Colony, where some of this book was written; to my research assistant Michael Vicario, a brilliant Shelley and Lucretius scholar who also knows a lot about motorcycles; to my editor Nancy Miller, whose gentle ruthlessness made this a far better book; and as always, to my friend and agent Gloria Loomis.